EDITOR: MARTIN WI...

OSPREY MILITARY

MEN-AT-ARMS

ARGENTINE ...
IN THE FALKLANDS

Text by
NICHOLAS VAN DER BIJL
Colour plates by
PAUL HANNON

Published in 1992 by
Osprey Publishing Ltd
59 Grosvenor Street, London W1X 9DA
© Copyright 1992 Osprey Publishing Ltd

ISBN 1 85532 227 7

Filmset in Great Britain
Printed through Bookbuilders Ltd, Hong Kong

Author's Note
The information in this text comes principally from
Argentinian sources including documentation, diaries,
photographs etc. The personal nature of this material
makes it inevitable that there will be some differences
between British and Argentinian accounts. To
compare incidents some reference has been made to:
Falklands The Air War, 1986, Arms and Armour Press,
Poole; *The Fight for the Malvinas*, 1989, Viking,
London.

THE GROUND WAR

The Argentinian Junta headed by General de Division Galtieri planned for an early summer invasion of the Falkland Islands Dependencies in early September 1982. However, a crisis developed in mid-March when a group of scrap-metal merchants landed at Leith in South Georgia and raised the Argentinian flag on what was British territory. This resulted in a flurry of diplomatic activity, and on 24 March a detachment of Royal Marines was landed at Gritvyken from HMS *Endurance*. The following day a small party of Buzo Tactico landed at Leith. More diplomatic activity ensued; but the Junta brought forward to 1 April the date of the operation, which would be codenamed Operation ROSARIO.

The Argentinian command then organised very quickly an invasion force, which left the mainland on 28 March. Taaska Fuerza (TF) 20 was the naval support force based around the cruiser *General Belgrano* and carrier *Vincente de Mayo*. TF 40 was the 900-strong Marine Infantry and Army assault force with immediate reinforcements; TF 60.1 was the force of 80 Marine Infantry designated to capture South Georgia. The plan was renamed Operation BLUE and, for the Falklands, called for an approach from the south-west. However a fierce gale blew up, which slowed down the approach; by early 2 April TF 40 was hove-to off Stanley. The landings proceeded, and Government House and the Royal Marine Barracks Moody Brook were captured after limited resistance. The following day South Georgia was captured after a short battle.

Formations

Meanwhile Britain had determined to despatch a Task Force to recover the lost territories. In Argentina, *Cuerpo Ejercito V*, responsible for the defence of Atlantic Litoral Theatre of Operations, despatched units to occupy the captured territory. Land Forces Argentine Occupied Territories was set up in Stanley and initially commanded by *Brigada de Infanteria IX* (Br I IX) with orders to defend the Falkland Islands against all attempts by Great Britain to recover them. Br I IX, with its Command Post at Moody Brook, began to arrive in strength. Regimiento de Infanteria 8 (RI 8) was sent to West Falkland and RI 25 remained on East Falkland, with a company at Goose Green. The invading Batallon de Infanteria Marina (2 BIM) defended the western sector of Stanley. The defence of the occupied territories was initially based on a series of platoon

strongpoints located around Stanley, Darwin peninsula and Fox Bay. The remainder was covered by foot, maritime and helicopter patrols.

When Great Britain despatched the Task Force, Br I X, occupying Chubut province south of Buenos Aires, prepared for deployment to the Falkland Islands. A massive programme, the Reinforcement Phase, commenced on 6 April to replace the new conscripts with reservists and to assemble equipment. *Brigada de Infanteria X* (Br I X) began re-deployment on 11 April. The following day Britain declared a Maritime Exclusion Zone (MEZ) of 200 miles from the centre of the Falkland Islands, declaring that any shipping inside the MEZ was liable to be attacked. The Argentinian Air Force established an air bridge to continue the reinforcement. By 16 April Br I X was near complete in the captured islands. The Marine Infantry presence was retained by placing 5 BIM on Mt Tumbledown.

With the arrival of Br I X there were now two brigades on the Falkland Islands, and a command and control problem to resolve. The newly established *Agrupacion Ejercito Malvinas* (Agr Ej Malvinas) selected the larger and more complete Br I X to

Two Ca Cdo Anf commandos light up after the British surrender. At their feet is equipment captured from NP 8901; in the background is a Royal Marines 4-ton Bedford. The right-hand man has tan brown leather SMG pouches.

2 April 1982: members of Ca Cdo Anf gather at Government House after the surrender of NP 8901. A variety of weapons can be seen including a 7.62mm 50.63 FAL with a skeletal folding butt (centre) and a 9mm Sterling (left). Those with the woollen balaclavas are Ca Cdo Anf; those with the distinctive berets are possibly Buzo Tactico, probably liaison personnel. The soldier in the foreground seems to have a small transceiver strapped across his stomach.

assume responsibility for the command of the ground forces, which it did, moving its Command Post to Stanley Town Hall. On 24 April *Brigada de Infanteria III* (Br I III) also began to reinforce Agr Ej Malvinas. The concept of defending the Stanley sector, leaving RI 25 around the airfield and deploying RIs 3 and 6 to overlook the southern beaches, remained. 5 BIM protected the routes from Darwin. RIs 4 and 7 faced north and west on Wireless Ridge, Mt Longdon, Two Sisters and Mt Wall, the so-called Outer Defence Zone. The mass of artillery and air defence was located on Stanley Common and around Stanley Airport. Br I IX assumed command for Falklands Litoral outside Stanley with regimental garrisons at Port Howard, Fox Bay and Goose Green, and company-sized groups eventually at Pebble Island and Port San Carlos. Several logistic difficulties in supplying the outlying garrisons were solved by using shipping, helicopters and heavy parachute drops.

On 26 April South Georgia was recaptured with the loss of 180 troops captured. On 30 April Britain declared a Total Exclusion Zone around the Falkland Islands. The 1 May air raids saw the opening rounds of the land campaign and although little damage was done, it did signal to the Argentinian garrison it was under siege. British Special Forces were also landed to gather intelligence. The following day the *Belgrano* was sunk, as was HMS *Sheffield* on 4 May. On 14 May the naval airstrip at Pebble Island was raided – the first confrontation, very limited though it was, between the opposing ground forces. The landings at San Carlos Water on 21 May led to direct contact at Port San Carlos, and then a week later at Goose Green, with the loss of the entire 1,200-strong garrison. A plan to move the headquarters of Br I IX to Goose Green was vetoed until the result of the battle was known. The Outer Defence Zone was straightened with the withdrawal of RI 4 to Mt Harriet. Two ineffective Special Forces operations were mounted in late April, the last one proving disastrous. By the beginning of June British patrols were probing the Outer Defence Zone in preparation for the assaults on RIs 4 and 7 and the eventual loss of both regiments. A day later Tumbledown and Wireless Ridge were attacked, which essentially destroyed the will of the Argentinians to continue.

With little hope of relief, in spite of valiant logistic efforts, Agr Ej Malvinas chose to surrender on 14 June 1982, with the loss of all its equipment. Some 12,980 Argentinians were captured, including at least 400 wounded; 16 officers, 35 NCOs and 148 conscript soldiers had been killed, and were later buried in the cemetery at San Carlos.

Agrupacion de Ejercito Malvinas Reserva Z

Agrupacion de Ejercito Malvinas Reserva Z (Reserva Z) was established on 7 April 1982. Initially drawn from Esc Exp C

Bl 181, it was located on the Racecourse with orders that it would be committed to Stanley, Fox Bay and Goose Green in that order. The lift would be Amphibious Force shipping or helicopters.

Within the week Reserva Z had been reinforced by a further armoured car unit, Esc Exp Bl 10, from Br I X, and an RI 6 roulement company. By the end of April, after the reinforcement phase, Reserva Z received definitive orders for the defence of Stanley. The two armoured car units were relocated to dominate the Estancia track. B/RI 6 occupied Two Sisters in support of RI 4 on Mt Wall. It was also warned to reinforce RI 6 and RI 3, in the event of approaches along the Fitzroy–Darwin road. In late April B/RI 12, Equipo Combate Solari (EC Solari) from B/RI 12, and A/RI 4 were attached to Reserva Z, bringing it to a regimental size grouping.

Agrupacion de Ejercito Malvinas wanted to commit Reserva Z against the San Carlos beachhead, but a pre-emptive British Harrier air strike early on 21 May against a helicopter hide east of Mt Kent precluded further operations. Thus Reserva Z remained where they were, undisturbed by the shelling of Stanley Common, but nevertheless exposed to the bitter weather, until 28 May. A strong detachment drawn from RI 12 echelon troops and the survivors of EC Guemes (see RI 25) were helicoptered to Goose Green and immediately committed. In answer to a further call for reinforcements, EC Solari were also lifted to south of Goose Green, but too late to influence the final result.

B/RI 6 performed well on Two Sisters but were forced to withdraw. On 12 June, A/RI 3 were transferred to Reserva Z to support 5 BIM on Mt Tumbledown or RI 7 on Mt Longdon and Wireless Ridge. B/RI 6 were then in reserve to 5 BIM, and made a spirited but unsuccessful counter-attack in the closing stages of the battle for Mt Tumbledown.

RI 7 were driven off Wireless Ridge by 2 Para, during which the two armoured car squadrons lent fire support. Esc Exp C Bl 10 also carried out an unsuccessful dismounted counter-attack up the ridge. A/RI 3 also attacked, but heavy fire destroyed this attempt, and the company retired covered by the guns of GA Aerot 4. This was the final Argentinian effort, and soon afterwards word was received of the surrender.

NAVAL & MARINE UNITS

Buzo Tactico

The Buzo Tactico, literally Tactical Divers, is a naval Special Forces unit based in Mar del Plata; similar to the United States SEALs, it specialises in beach and coastal recce and underwater demolition.

There is some evidence that a small Buzo Tactico detachment accompanied the civilian scrap metal merchants to Leith on South Georgia, arriving on the *Bahia Paraiso* on 19 March 1982. They took military equipment but remained dressed in civilian clothes.

During the invasion of the Falkland Islands a 12-man Buzo Tactico team was landed from the submarine *Santa Fe* and established that the Yorke Bay beaches were clear of enemy and obstacles. They then activated navigation beacons for the assault force. Their task complete, they returned to Argentina within the day. Buzo Tactico were mistakenly credited with the capture of Government House and Royal Marine Party 8901; this seems to have been a journalistic error, since Ca Cdo Anf were responsible.

Meanwhile on South Georgia, the *Bahia Paraiso* and the Type 69 frigate *Guerrico* forming Task Force 60.1 arrived off Grytviken on 2 April. Seeing that it was occupied by a Royal Marine detachment from HMS *Endurance*, the ships returned to pick up the Buzo Tactico, who were at Leith with a 1 BIM platoon. Early on 3 April the assault force landed, but after some fighting a stalemate situation developed and the British, with no hope of relief, were forced to surrender.

It is likely that some Buzo Tactico were captured when South Georgia was retaken on 25 April.

Batallon de Infanteria Marina 1

Batallon de Infanteria Marina 1 (1 BIM), part of Brigada de

Falkland Islanders pass B Veh Anf LVTP-7 Amtracs soon after the surrender. Note the national insignia and Marine forces anchor and rope on the side of the vehicles: see also Osprey Vanguard 45, Amtracs, Plate G.

A group of senior officers escort Marine Infantry commander Rear-Admiral Büsser, in camouflaged uniform, in Stanley. Also evident is an officer each from the FAA, Navy and Army. From left to right; Brig.Gen. L. Castellano, commander of IX Air Brigade; Maj. Gen. Osvaldo J. Garcia, commander TOM; and extreme right, Rear-Admiral G. O. Allara, Commander of Task Forces 40 and 79. A Navy rating follows, left background.

Glossary of Terms

Aerot	Aereotransportado	Airborne
ADA	Aerea defensa	Air defence
Ag	Agrupacion	(Army) Group
Am	Ametralladoras	Machine gun
Amtrac		amphibious tracked vehicle
Anf	Anfibios	Amphibious
BAM	Base Aerea Militar	Military Air Base
BIM	Batallon Infanteria Marina	Marine Infantry Bn.
Br	Brigada	Brigade
Ca	Compania	Company
Cam	Campana	Field
C Bl	Caballeria Blindada	Armoured recce/car
comm	Communicacion	Signals
Col	Coronel	Colonel
	Cuerpo	Corps
EAN	Estacion Aerea Naval	Naval Air Station
EC	Equipo Combate	Combat team
Ej	Ejercito	Army
Esc	Escuadron	Squadron
	Escuala	School
Ex	Exploracion	Recce
FAA	Fuerza Armada Argentina	Argentinian Air Force
FE	Fuerza Especial	Special Forces
FT	Fuerza Taaska	Task Force

Ga	Grupo de Artilleria	Artillery group
GC	Grupo de Casa	Home defence
Gen de Br	General de Brigada	Brigadier
Gen de Div	General de Division	Major-General
GN	Gendarmerie Nacional	National Guard
IM	Infanteria Marina	Marine Infantry
Ing	Ingenerios	Engineer
Int	Intelligencia	Intelligence
Log	Logistique	Logistic
LST	Landing Ship Tank	
LVTP	Landing Vehicle Tracked Personnel	
Maint	Maintaineros	Maintenance
Maj	Mayor	Major
Mec	Mecanizada	Mechanised
OE	Operaciones especiales	Special operations
PM	Policia Militar	Military Police
PNA	Prefectura Naval Argentina	Argentinian Coastguard
Pr Tte	Primero Teniente	First lieutenant
RI	Regimiento de Infanteria	Infantry regiment
San	Sanidad	Medical
Sec Tte	Secundo Teniente	Second lieutenant
Tte	Teniente	Lieutenant
Tte Col	Teniente Coronel	Lieutenant-Colonel

Infanteria Marina 1 and normally based in Tierra del Fuego, contributed a platoon-sized grouping to seize South Georgia. This was embarked on the Type 69 frigate *Guerrico*, which formed part of Task Force 60.1 assigned to capture South Georgia then occupied by a small group of Royal Marines. On 3 April the force hove-to off Grytviken and the Marine Infantry were taken ashore in a B Av C 601 Puma and a Navy Alouette. The Royal Marine defenders shot down the Puma and damaged the *Geurrico*; the Alouette continued to ferry troops ashore. Both sides held an advantage with the Royal Marines well dug in but without hope of relief and the Marine Infantry platoon, although supported by a damaged warship, waiting for reinforcements. The British elected to surrender. 1 BIM lost two killed in the battle of Grytviken. They then accompanied their Royal Marine prisoners back to Argentina on board *Bahia Paraiso*.

Batallon de Infanteria Marina 2

Early on 28 March Task Force 40, the amphibious element of the Armada Argentina Task Force 20 assigned to recapture the Falkland Islands, slipped out of Puerto Belgrano and headed into the Atlantic Ocean. Among the troops on board the LST *Cabo San Antonio* were the 390 men of the Batallon de Infanteria Marina (2 BIM) divided into three rifle companies with the normal headquarters and support elements. The force ran into a severe gale which caused the original plan to approach the Falkland Islands from the south-east to be rejected in favour of a northerly approach. Early on 2 April the *Cabo San Antonio* took up a position about two miles off Pembroke Head.

Soon after the Buzo Tactico divers had cleared the beaches, 2 BIM climbed into the B Veh Anf/IM LVTP-7s and LARC-5s and in three waves headed toward Yorke Bay. Ashore and firm, 2 BIM advanced towards Stanley, encountering no enemy until the outskirts of the town, when the leading vehicles came under fire. The Marine Infantry quickly assaulted the position to find it abandoned. The column moved through Stanley, the Amtracs over-revving to give an impression of numbers. No further resistance was encountered.

The leading company moved on towards Government House, where unexpected resistance had been encountered. They linked up with a Ca Anf Cdo patrol also reinforcing the attack on Government House, but arrived as negotiations for the surrender of the British had begun. 2 BIM then took up defensive positions around Wireless Ridge and Cortley Hill with A/BACM 1 in support on Stanley Common. Within a fortnight 2 BIM handed over to RI 7 and returned to Puerto Belgrano.

Batallon de Infanteria Marina 3

On 24 April Compania H (H/3 BIM) were flown to Stanley to guard naval installations on the Falkland Islands. Three days later the first platoon and a detachment Ca Ing Anf/IM flew to Pebble Island to establish Estacion Aerea Naval Calderon. Over the next few days more equipment arrived, including aircraft. The second platoon remained in Stanley, while the third deployed on security duties at the Cortley Hill fuel dump.

On 1 May, British air strikes on the airfields at Stanley and Goose Green forced their closure and six FAA Pucara were ordered to fly to Pebble Island. The worsening weather forced the closure of EAN Calderon to fixed-wing aircraft on 5 May, isolating several aircraft. The health of the Marine Infantry was also causing concern.

Pebble Island then became of interest to the British and on 14 May was raided by D/22 SAS. The Marine Infantry first knew

Major-General Osvaldo J. Garcia, Commander TOM, speaking at the victory ceremony. Note the gorget patches and 'two-sun' pocket ranking.

something was amiss when reports were received that a number of aircraft had caught fire. A fire-fighting party then ran into an unexpected hail of fire and wisely withdrew. In purely military terms, the raid was a total success, nine aircraft being written off or damaged.

Over the following weeks the garrison witnessed several air-to-air combats, hosted shot down Argentinian pilots, and recovered the bodies of others. They also saw the devastating Skyhawk attack on HMS *Coventry* and *Broadsword*. On 28 May the platoon assisted with the casualty evacuation of sick and wounded on a FAA Twin Otter that arrived from the mainland. Not to be outdone, two Navy Sea Kings also casevacuated Navy personnel.

On 10 June the garrison received orders from Cdo/3 BIM to prepare to move to Port Howard. Two days later the hospital ship *Bahia Paraiso* arrived and took off the sick. On 15 June the Pebble Island garrison, about 155 all ranks, surrendered and were transported to the prison camp at Ajax Bay. For the islanders their ordeal, no less stressful than that of the inhabitants of Goose Green, was over.

Meanwhile 3/H/2 BIM, protecting fuel near Cortley Hill, had experienced a quiet time. Reinforced by B/GADA 101, they witnessed the shelling and bombing across Stanley inner harbour. On 14 June British Special Forces, having sped across from

Gen. Galtieri, the leader of the Junta , and Brig. Gen. O. L. Joffre, Commander X Brigade, then Land Forces Commander Falklands, walk together on Stanley Common. Note Galtieri's rank insignia *worn on both the parka and tunic pocket, and national cockade worn on his unusual winter officer's cap. Joffre wears tan brushed cotton gloves and carries a silver-topped baton.*

Cochon Island, attempted a landing below Cortley Hill to raid the fuel tanks. The Marine Infantry retaliated, and the attack quickly dissolved as the raiders withdrew under a hail of small arms and artillery fire redirected from the Wireless Ridge battle.

Batallon de Infanteria Marina 5

Batallon de Infanteria Marina 5 (5 BIM) was organic to 1st Fleet Marine Force and based at Rio Grande. The unit had a standard organisation of headquarters, support and service support elements, three Marine Infantry companies, each company numbering 150 all ranks divided into three platoons of three sections.

5 BIM were flown to the Falkland Islands in late April and were immediately assigned to Sector BRONCE (bronze) of the Inner Defence Ring, based around Mt Tumbledown, Mt William and Sapper Hill. With the assistance of Ca Ing Anf/IM, field defences were hacked out of the rocky outcrops. Batterie B, Batallon de Artilleria de Campana de Marina 1 (B/BACM 1) provided artillery support. For air defence the Marine Infantry were reliant on the unit's twelve M2 0.50 Browning machine guns, although these would be supplemented by Ca Am 12.7/IM's machine guns.

N/5 BIM was on Mt Tumbledown, M/5 BIM on Mt William and O/5 BIM in a blocking position to the south. The Marine

Infantry seem to have coped reasonably well with the hostile conditions, although there is some evidence that they were given privileges, organised through Marine channels, denied to the Army units. 5 BIM saw little direct action until mid-June, although some casualties were taken in May during the naval and air bombardment of Stanley Common. When the Outer Defence Zone was attacked on 12 June, 5 BIM arranged for B/BACM 1 to provide covering fire for RI 4, heavily engaged on Mt Harriet. When the feature fell some withdrawing troops, including B/RI 6 from Reserva Z, were absorbed into the order of battle. Esc Exp 181 and A/RI 3 were held as reinforcements in readiness between Tumbledown and Wireless Ridge.

Battle of Mt Tumbledown

2nd Scots Guards (2SG) were selected to attack Mt Tumbledown and were helicoptered from Goose Green to Goat Ridge. The attack began during the night of 13 June. O/5 BIM were alert to any approaches from the west and their vigilance was rewarded when a diversionary attack was forced to retire in some confusion. On Mt William Cdo/5 BIM were confident that the British attack had been defeated.

Meanwhile 2SG had secured initial objectives on the western slopes of Tumbledown, but a brisk fight developed as the Guardsmen tried to breach the Argentinian defences. For four hours the battle raged, the British pinned down by accurate artillery fire and barely able to move in the freezing night; but 5 BIM were gradually prised off the ridge as 2SG seized the initiative, and overwhelmed the defenders in a series of co-ordinated attacks. Even when the British reached the summit of Tumbledown there was a violent scuffle before the defenders were driven off. A weak local counter-attack was driven off. A counter-attack by B/RI 6, in reserve, initially made ground but was driven off the ridge and withdrew to Stanley. The defence cost 10 Marine Infantry and 16 Army killed, missing and wounded, and the fighting had lasted seven hours. A composite Army/Marine Infantry platoon took 50 per cent casualties.

Battle of Sapper Hill

On Sapper Hill, Cdo/5 BIM, M/5 BIM and some survivors from the fighting of the night remained firm. The 1st Welsh Guards (1WG) group, with 40 and 45 Commando, were ordered to seize Sapper Hill. The Marine Infantry were astounded when three Sea King helicopters dropped Royal Marines on a track below them. A brisk firefight developed, resulting in the deaths of three Marine Infantry, the last to be killed in the war.

Meanwhile 1/7 Gurkha Rifles were ordered to assault Mt William and moved off in the gathering light, taking a track to the north of Tumbledown; but before any tactical moves were made, word was received that the Argentinians were surrendering. 5 BIM were assembled and marched to Stanley Airport, and after a lengthy wait the majority were repatriated to Argentina on 21 June.

Batallon de Artilleria de Campana de Marina 1

Bateria A, Battalon de Artilleria de Campana de Marina 1 (A/BACM 1) traditionally operated with 2 BIM and thus formed part of the 2 April invasion force. Equipped with six Italian M56 105mm Oto Melara pack howitzers, it was deployed onto Stanley Common to support 2 BIM digging-in on Mt Longdon, Two Sisters and Mt Harriet. When RI 7 took over this position in mid-April, A/BACM 1 also returned to Argentina with its guns.

B/BACM 1, also with six M56, arrived with its traditional

hosts, 5 BIM, in late April and replaced A/BACM 1 on Stanley Common, with the majority of the artillery, to support the Marine Infantry on Mt Tumbledown.

During the battle for Tumbledown the Marine gunners provided valuable support for 0/5 BIM, manning a blocking position south-west of Tumbledown, during its engagement with a British diversionary attack on the track to Fitzroy. During the battle for Mt Tumbledown the battery also provided accurate close support for the hard-pressed Army and Marine Infantry. Indeed, each time the shelling started both sides took cover until it lifted and then firefights began again. The battery passed into captivity, along with its guns, although two conscript gunners had been killed by the offshore shelling.

Compania de Commando Anfibios

Companie de Commando Anfibios (Ca Cdo Anf) is a small Special Forces unit based in Mar del Plata, with a role similar to the British Special Boat Service.

On 28 March Task Force 40 slipped out of Buenos Aires and in the face of deteriorating weather turned south. The 35-strong Ca Cdo Anf settled down into the routine of Embarked Force life on the Type 42 destroyer *Santissima Trinidad*. At dusk on 1 April the warship hove-to about a mile south of Mullet Creek. The company divided into two detachments, the smaller one to seize Government House and the larger one to neutralise the Royal Marine Barracks at Moody Brook. After several delays, Ca Cdo Anf Company struggled ashore near Lake Point.

The 'going' was difficult. A Royal Marine observation post was bypassed, and it was not until the early morning that the larger column arrived at Moody Brook Barracks. They called for surrender and, although there was no sign of life, the Marines stormed the buildings and then settled into defensive positions.

The smaller detachment reached Government House and noted the presence of troops in the area. The Marines were not to know that they had stumbled on the main defensive position of Royal Marine Naval Party 8901 (NP 8901) and were outnumbered by about 31 to 15. Nevertheless, the team decided to stick to the original plan of simply demanding the surrender of the Governor. This failed, and a short action ensued. A 'snatch' squad entered the servants' quarters and came under heavy fire which cut down the commander, wounded another and forced the remaining three back inside, where they were eventually captured. The wounded officer lay dying in the garden. The first attempt to storm Government House had failed and the detachment at Moody Brook was summoned to reinforce the assault. It was met by the Amtrac-borne 2 BIM, but arrived as the sporadic firing died down and surrender negotiations started. The defenders filed out to be taken prisoner by Ca Cdo Anf.

Within the day Ca Cdo Anf had returned to Argentina, taking with them the body of their commander. An accident of public relations had later to credit the Buzo Tactico for this operation carried out by the Marine Commandos.

Batallon de Vehiclos Anfibios

Batallon de Vehiclos Anfibios (B Veh Anf), part of the Argent-

Grouped around a penguin are five infantry conscripts. Clearly visible on the upper arm of the right-hand soldier is the national flash of Argentina. Three carry the 7.62mm FAL 50.00 semi-automatic rifle.

This soldier wears the Argentinian version of the British Army 'heavy duty sweater'. The Red Ensign is displayed on a 7.62mm FAL 50.63 with folding skeletal butt and green leather sling.

Browning nine-gun sections, each consisting of three 'grupos' of 13 Marine Infantry per weapon. Each 'grupo' consisted of a gun team and local defence.

Ca Am 12.7/IM arrived in late April, and sections were deployed with RI 7 on Mt Longdon and with RI 4 on Mt Harriet and Two Sisters; the remainder were sent to Cortley Ridge to join the third platoon of H/3 BIM. All teams saw action and quickly gained the respect of the British for their accuracy and rate of fire. The company lost seven killed.

ARMY UNITS

Regimiento de Infanteria 1

In mid-April Regimiento de Infanteria 1 (RI 1), 'Los Patricios', the oldest unit in the Argentinian Army, was detailed to select a company to reinforce the Falkland Islands. The regiment is based in Buenos Aires, and apart from its combat role provides infantry for ceremonial occasions.

By 13 April its A/RI 1 had been assembled and was flown to Stanley, where it joined RI 6 on Stanley Common. It was then redesignated C/RI 6 and replaced the RI 6 company that rotated through the Agrupacion Ejercito Malvinas reserve. The Ca PM 181 detachment, which was a temporary infantry reinforcement, returned to Stanley Police Station. On 8 June a 100-strong squadron from Regimiento de Grenaderos de General San Martin arrived, bringing several MAG teams, and was detached to A/RI 1. One section was sent to support RI 4 on Mt Harriet and was subsequently captured when the feature fell. A/RI 1 did not experience any combat but was exposed to the air and naval pounding of Stanley Common by the British.

Regimiento de Infanteria 3

Regimiento de Infanteria 3 (RI 3) was one of three major components of Br I III, along with RIs 6 and 7. Numbering 930 all ranks, it was divided into three rifle companies, a headquarters and a service company.

RI 3 arrived in mid-April and was assigned Sector ORO (gold) to cover the southern beaches and possible helicopter landing sites. Ca Ing 601 provided a detachment to assist in the defences; a Forward Observation Party was assigned from GA 3 and four Esc Exp Cl B 181 Panhards were attached as armoured support. The regiment remained static throughout the campaign and was subjected to much naval shelling and frequent air attack. Casualties mounted, particularly psychological, and the supply system failed.

On the night of 13 June A/RI 3 was detached to Reserva Z ready to reinforce 5 BIM on Mt Tumbledown or RI 7 on Wireless Ridge. 5 BIM did not use the company, but RI 7 called for it to regain Wireless Ridge; this attack failed in spite of several attempts. The troops withdrew under covering fire from GA Aerot 4.

RI 3 surrendered soon afterwards, and after a short stay at the airfield was repatriated to Argentina. Some officers were retained as prisoners until July. RI 3 was not a happy regiment, and the CO was to comment later that their 60 days in foxholes destroyed their will to fight.

inian Amphibious Support Force, provided amphibious support to the Marine Infantry and was equipped with US-manufactured LVTP-7 and LARC-5 amphibious tracked vehicles (Amtracs). Its base is Puerto Belgrano.

By 28 March the unit had been loaded onto the LST *Cabo San Antonio*, which then headed out into the Atlantic Ocean. After negotiating a severe storm the vessel hove-to on 2 April about two miles north of Pembroke Head. The sea was calm. The landings, in three waves, went according to plan, although the Marine commander of the operation came ashore in reverse gear when his Amtrac refused to engage first forward. While the C/RI 25 platoon seized the Airport, 2 BIM advanced towards Stanley, the Amtrac drivers over-revving the engines to deceive defenders that the force was larger than it was. On the outskirts of Stanley the leading vehicle was laced by accurate machine-gun fire. The Marine Infantry immediately counter-attacked to find the position abandoned. B Veh Anf clattered through Stanley towards Moody Brook. West of Government House the Amtracs met a Ca Cdo Anf detachment on their way to Government House, where unexpected resistance had been met. The Marine Commandos were loaded on top of the Amtracs and arrived as surrender was being negotiated.

The battalion remained in Stanley for a few days, but the deployment of the Amtracs proved almost useless; an attempt to drive to Estancia failed when the vehicles became bogged. Within a fortnight of the invasion. B Veh Anf had returned to Argentina.

Compania de Ametralladoras 12.7/Infanteria Marina

Compania de Ametralladoras 12.7/Infanteria Marina (Ca Am 12.7/IM) was a 120-strong composite unit drawn from 1 BIM, based in Puerto Belgrano, and Batallon de Commando, based in Rio Santiago. Its principal role was to reinforce 5 BIM in covering helicopter landing sites with long-range suppressive machine-gun fire. It was organised into three M2 0.50 (12.7mm)

Formation/Unit/Detachment	Commander	Deployment
Agrupacion de Ejercito Malvinas		
Special Forces		
Compania de Commando 601 (Ca Cdo 601)	Maj Mario Castenago	
Compania de Commando 602 (Ca Cdo 602)	Maj Aldo Rico	
Compania de Fuerzas Especial 601 de Gendarmerie Nacional (Ca FE 601 GN)		
Cavalry		
Escuadron de Exploracion Caballeria		Stanley environs
Blindada 181 (Esc Exp C Bl 181)		Reserva Z
Los Regimiento de Grenaderos de General		with RI 1
San Martin		Outer Defence Zone
Artillery and Air Defence		
Grupo de Artilleria Aereotransportado 4		Stanley Common
(GA Aerot 4)		Goose Green
Grupo de Aerea Defensa 601 (GADA 601)	Tte Col Hector Arias	Stanley environs
		Goose Green
Grupo de Aerea Defensa 602 (GADA 602)		
Combat and Service Support		
Compania de Ingenieros de Combate 601	Maj Jorge Etienot	Stanley
601 (Ca Ing 601)		
Grupo de Aviacion de Combate 601	Tte Col Juan Scarpa	Stanley environs
(Ca Av C 601)		
Compania de Aerea Maintaineros 601		Stanley environs
(Ca Ae Maint 601)		
Compania de Communicacion 181 (Ca Comm 181)	Tte Col Andujar	
Compania de Policia Militar 181 (Ca PM 181)	Maj Roberto Berazay	Stanley
Compania de Inteligencia 181 (Ca Int 181)		Stanley
Compania de Logistique de Constructiones 601	Col Arnaldo Busso	Stanley
(Ca Log Const 601)		
Brigada de Infanteria III (Br I III)	**Gen de Br Parada**	Falkland environs
Regimiento de Infanteria 4 (RI 4)	Tte Col Diego Soria	Outer Defence Zone
Regimiento de Infanteria 5 (RI 5)	Col Juan R. Mabranga	Port Howard
Regimiento de Infanteria 12 (RI 12)	Tte Col Italo Piaggi	Goose Green
Grupo de Artilleria 3 (GA 3)	Tte Col Martin Balsa	Stanley Common
Grupo de Artilleria 101 (GA 101)		Stanley
Batallon de Logistique 3 (B Log 3)		
Compania de Ingenerios de Combate 3 (Ca Ing 3)	Major Oscar Lima	
Compania de Comunicacion 3 (Ca Comm 3)		
Brigada de Infanteria IX (Br I IX)	**Gen de Br Daher**	
Batallon de Infanteria 8 (RI 8)	Tte Col Ernesto Repossi	Fox Bay
Batallon de Infanteria 25 (RI 25)	Tte Col Mohammad	Stanley Airport
	Seineilden	Port San Carlos
Batallon de Logistique 9 (B Log 9)		Stanley
		Goose Green
Compania de Ingenerios de Combate 9	Maj Luis Lima	Fox Bay
(Ca Ing 9)		Goose Green
Compania de Communicacion 9 (Ca Comm 9)		Stanley
		Fox Bay
		Port Howard
Compania de Sanidad 9 (Ca San 9)		Fox Bay
Brigada de Infanteria Mecanizada X (Br I X)	**Gen de Br Joffre**	Stanley sector
Regimiento de Infanteria Mecanizado 3 (RI 3)	Tte Col David Comini	Stanley Common
Regimiento de Infanteria Mecanizado 6 (RI 6)	Tte Col Jorge Halperin	Stanley Common

continued overleaf

Table A: Assessed Argentinian Order of Battle 2 April – 14 June 1982

Formation/Unit/Detachment	Commander	Deployment
Regimiento de Infanteria Mecanizado 7 (RI 7)	Tte Col Ortiz Gimenez	Mt Longdon
Compania A, Regimiento de Infanteria 1 (A/RI 1)	Pr Tte MacDonado	Stanley Common
Grupo de Artilleria Aereotransportado 4 (GA Aerot 4)	Tte Col Carlos Quevedo	Stanely Common Goose Green
Batallon de Logistique 10 Mecanizada (B Log 10)		
Escuadron de Exploracion Caballeria Blindada 10 (Esc Exp C Bl 10)	Maj Alejandro Carullo	
Compania de Ingenieros Mecanizda 10 (Ca Ing 10)	Maj Carlos Matalon	Stanely environs
Compania de Communicacion Mecanizado 10 (Ca Comm 10)	Maj Juan Tomatis	Stanley
Compania de Operaciones Electronicios Mecanizado 10 (Ca OE 10)		
Compania de Sanidad Mecanizado 10 (Ca San 10)		

Armada Argentina and Infanteria Marina

Formation/Unit/Detachment	Commander	Deployment
Detachment Buzo Tactico	Tte Alfredo Astiz	S Georgia Invasion
1 × Platoon Batallon de Infanteria Marina 1 (1 BIM)	Tte Guillermo Luna	S Georgia
Batallon de Infanteria Marina 2 (2 BIM)	Cdr Alfredo Weinstubel	Invasion Mt Longdon
Compania H, Batallon de Infanteria Marina (H/3 BIM)	Tte Marega	Pebble Island Cortley Hill Stanley
Batallon de Infanteria Marina 5 (5 BIM)	Tte Col Carlos Robacio	Mt Tumbledown
Batterie A Batallon de Artilleria de Campana Infanteria Marina (A/B Art Cam/IM)	Tte Mario Perez	with 2 BIM
Batterie B Batallon de Artilleria de Campana Infanteria Marina (B/B Art Cam/IM)	Sec Tte Mario Abadal	with 5 BIM
Compania de Commando Anfibios (Ca Cdo Anf)	Ltd Cdr Sanchez Sabarots	Invasion
Batallon de Antiaerea/Infanteria Marina (B A/IM)	Lt Cdr Hector Silva	Stanley Airport
Compania de Ingenerios Anfibios/Infanteria Marina (Ca Ing/IM)	Lt Cdr Luis Meghini	Dispersed
Compania se Ametralladoras 12.7/Infanteria Marina (Ca Am12.7/IM)	Sec Tte Sergio Dacharry	Dispersed

Fuerza Aerea Argentina

Formation/Unit/Detachment	Commander	Deployment
Grupo 2 VYCA/Escuadron 2 VYCA Malvinas		
Escuadron 1 and 2, Grupo de Artilleria Antiaereapi (Rh 202s)		Stanley environs Goose Green
Grupo de Operaciones Especiales (GOE)		Special Forces
Equipo Control de Combate Organisacion (ECCO)		Special Forces
Escuala de Militar Aviacion		Goose Green Special operations

Agrupacion de Ejercito Malvinas Reserva Z (commitments)

Formation/Unit/Detachment	Commander	Deployment
Esc Exp C Bl 181		Moody Brook
Esc C Bl 10		Wireless Ridge
RI 6 roulement coy		B/RI 6 — Two Sisters Mt Tumbledown
B/RI 12 (EC SOLARI)		Goose Green
A/RI 3		Wireless Ridge
A/RI 4		Stanley environs

Task Forces and Combat Teams:

Formation/Unit/Detachment	Commander	Deployment
Fuerza Taaska Mercedes	Tte Col Piaggi	Goose Green
RI 12 (–)		
C/RI 25		
Platoon RI 8		
A/GA Aerot 4 (3 × M56 out of 4 operational)		
3/B/GADA 601 (GDF-002)		

continued

Formation/Unit/Detachment	Commander	Deployment
Fuerza Taaska Caseros		Blocakde relief columns
Cdo/RI 4		
B/RI 4		
C/RI 4		
A/GA Aerot 4		
Fuerza Taaska Reconquistado	**Col Mabranga**	Port Howard
RI 8		
Ca Ing 3(–)		
Ca Comm 3(–)		
Ca San 3(–)		
Equipo Combate Guemes		Port San Carlos
Composite platoon drawn from C/RI 25	Pr Tte Carlos Etsaban	
EC Solari		Mt Harriet and Goose Green
B/RI 12	Capt Eduardo Consiglia	
EC 25 de Mayo		
C/RI 25 (–)		

Regimiento de Infanteria 4

In 1982 Regimiento de Infanteria 4 (RI 4) was a major component of Br I IX and was based near Corrientes, on the northern borders of Argentina. Its 800 troops were divided into the standard three rifle companies, supported by a headquarters and support elements.

RI 4 arrived on the Falkland Islands on 27 April, minus a substantial amount of heavy equipment. A/RI 4 was immediately detached to Reserva Z and protected a area around Mt Low while the remainder of the regiment marched to Mt Wall. Digging-in proved very difficult, but a series of sangars sprouted amongst the rocks. The troops were soon suffering from the hostile weather and the poor logistic chain. Some patrolling was done and Mt Challenger occupied. B/RI 12, EC Solari, then with Reserva Z, joined RI 4 to replace A/RI 4; but on 28 May all but one platoon was flown to Goose Green, where it was sucked into the capitulation of RI 12.

In late May a series of significant actions took place. Contact was made with a Ca Cdo 602 patrol that had managed to survive encirclement by British advanced forces, and Intelligence confirmed the enemy approach on Stanley on two axes. RI 4 was therefore pulled back to the Outer Defence Zone and occupied

An unidentified unit on parade, but possibly C/RI 25 at San Carlos. Note the bugler (second left) with his instrument tucked under his right arm. All wear ALICE waistbelts and yokes with Argentinian leather pouches. Note the thick woollen gloves. The helmets have US 'woodland'-style camouflaged covers.

An infantry platoon, possibly from RI 25, formally march past. The right-hand marker carries a US M20 3.5in 'Super Bazooka' anti-tank rocket launcher. The fourth man along the front rank carries a 7.62mm MAG general purpose machine gun on his right shoulder.

Two Sisters and Mt Harriet. The British then established an OP on Mt Wall, which reported every move of RI 4. Reinforcements arrived, including Ca Ing 10 and Ca Ing Anf/IM. Throughout early June RI 4 held its own in a series of patrol actions as the British prepared to attack the Outer Defence Zone.

Battle of Two Sisters

45 Commando were assigned to attack Two Sisters, and decided on a silent approach. The 120 soldiers from C/RI 4, on the western peak, and B/RI 6, on the eastern peak, were alerted by the assault on Mt Longdon by 3 Para. 45 Cdo secured a foothold on the western slopes, and C/RI 4 disintegrated in the face of a wild charge by Z/45 Cdo. Most conscripts filtered into Stanley, although some joined 5 BIM on Mt Tumbledown. B/RI 6 nearly fought Y/45 Cdo to a standstill in some rugged fighting, but were ordered to abandon their positions. They filed off in good order and took up a position to support 5 BIM. Eight soldiers were killed and 54 taken prisoner.

Battle of Mt Harriet

42 Cdo were ordered to capture Mt Harriet from the south, and then to exploit through to Goat Ridge. On the feature, B/RI 4, Cdo/RI 4, a B/RI 12 platoon and a Seccion de Defensa Br I III (Sec Def/Br I III) were alerted by the fighting to the north. However, the leading Royal Marine companies managed to reach their forward positions undetected and assaulted. The B/RI 12 platoon, in the centre of the position, was swept aside by K/42 Cdo, who then struck westwards to assault B/RI 4 on the western peak. The Sec Def/Br I III was destroyed by L/42 Cdo, who then wheeled right to assault Cdo/RI 4 on the eastern summit. Argentinian communications failed. A 16-man MAG team from

Regimiento de Grenaderos de General San Martin gave covering fire to B/RI 4, who were destroyed in a belated counter-attack, although one platoon did reach 5 BIM.

Some 250 soldiers were taken prisoners, including CO RI 4, and about 10 Argentinians were killed. The survivors were received in Stanley with disdain and contempt. The regiment was sent to the prison camp at Fox Bay and then, when the Argentinians surrendered, transferred to Stanley Airfield. The majority were quickly repatriated, although several officers were retained as prisoners until early July.

Regimiento de Infanteria 6

Regimiento de Infanteria 6 (RI 6), with its sister units RI 3 and RI 7, was in 1982 a major component of Br I X and based in the Mercedes area of Buenos Aires province. Organisation was standard with three rifle companies, command, and service and support company-sized groupings.

RI 6 arrived on 14 April and took up positions on Stanley Common, in Sector ACERO (steel), with orders to cover the southern approaches. Ca Ing 10 assisted with the construction of field defences and the laying of minefields, and a Ca PM 181 detachment was also assigned as infantry reinforcement to replace C/RI 6, which had been temporarily detached to Reserva Z. RI 6 was also tasked with the co-ordination of the Army air defence of Stanley Common. In mid-April A/RI 1 joined RI 6, was designated C/RI 6, and replaced the Ca PM 181 detachment.

The bad weather took its toll of the conscripts, whose shelters and tents were often blown down by the wind. Weapons became defective. On 25 April RI 6 was ordered to detach roulement companies to Reserva Z. B/RI 6 and the snipers were sent to Two Sisters to support RI 4 on Mt Wall, while heliborne patrols carried out a census in the larger settlements.

Life on Stanley Common was very stressful and the difficulties were often compounded by inaccurate rumour. The jamming of the regiment's radios was a constant reminder that the British were not far away. Air defence arrangements suffered a severe blow when a four-man Roland team were killed within the unit's

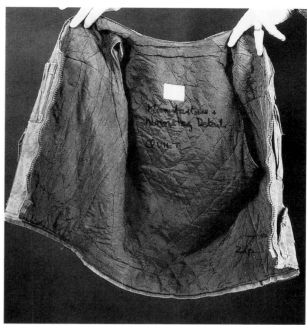

A Marine Infantry combat waistcoat. Specialist pockets were used for the storage of a compass (right shoulder), combat knife (under right arm), pistol (under left arm), magazines (left waistband) and two large pockets on reverse for large items. The inside is quilted.

lines by a shell. Unfortunately many gun positions were in the RI 6 lines, and consequently the infantrymen came under counter-battery fire. In early June RI 6 despatched two 120mm Thompson Brandt mortars and six 7.62mm MAG teams to support 5 BIM and RI 7. B/RI 6 became involved in the battle for Two Sisters and withdrew in good order. They were then placed under command of 5 BIM, and counter-attacked during the final stages of the fight for Mt Tumbledown, but failed to reach their objective.

The final night of the war, 13 June, was a nightmare for the conscripts, the discomfort being made even worse when GA 101 set up its fire control centre near the RI 6 Command Post; and news of the surrender was thus received with some relief. RI 6 passed into captivity, and were repatriated within the week to Argentina on SS *Canberra*. Some officers remained as prisoners until early July.

Regimiento de Infanteria 7

Regimiento de Infanteria 7 (RI 7) was, in 1982, a major unit of Br I X, and was based in La Tablada in the province of Buenos Aires. It numbered a mix of 700 recalled reservists, new conscripts, and those nearing the end of their two years' National Service. Organisation was conventional with three rifle companies, a service and support company and a headquarters element.

By 13 April, RI 7 had been flown to the Falkland Islands to relieve 2 BIM on Mt Longdon and Wireless Ridge in Sector PLATA (silver). A Ca Ing 10 detachment was assigned for sapper tasks. Esc Exp C Bl 10 and Esc Exp C Bl 181 were in support from Reserva Z. GA 3 was on call from Br I X.

RI 7 held the right flank of the Outer Defence Zone. B/RI 7, a Ca Ing 10 detachment and a Ca Am 12.7/IM sections were placed on Mt Longdon, the main defensive position centring on the summit. Support weapons covered the entire ridge. A/ and C/RI 7 were placed on Wireless Ridge, facing north and west. A platoon was placed on a small feature to the north-east. Cdo/RI 7 was at Moody Brook. Digging-in was difficult, but sangars and bunkers with interlocking arcs of fire were established on both features. Life was not idyllic, and resupply difficult. Harrier strikes caused some damage, although small arms fire damaged aircraft on successive days.

Battle of Mt Longdon

During the night of 12/13 June Mt Longdon was assaulted by 3 Para. Their silent approach compromised when a mine exploded, A/3 Para's attempt to climb the northern slopes was defeated. B/3 Para established a precarious foothold on the western summit. The ridge was narrow and the battle swept to and fro for several hours, at one stage Ca Ing 10 regaining lost ground. It was only when a key machine-gun position was destroyed in a lone action that the defence began to dissolve; defensive emplacements and strongpoints were systematically destroyed, the defenders losing about 25 killed and 50 taken prisoner. About half the garrison reached Wireless Ridge. An A/RI 7 platoon counter-attacked, but failed.

Battle of Wireless Ridge

2 Para were selected for the assault on Wireless Ridge. To support the attack, the battalion could rely on substantial artillery, a frigate and a troop of the Blues & Royals with Scorpion

and Scimitar armoured vehicles. Shortly after dark on 13 June the platoon on a small feature to the north of Wireless Ridge was overwhelmed; A/ and B/2 Para then captured another small feature to the north-west of the main objective, and the main assault began. D/2 Para soon became entangled among the boulders as RI 7 stubbornly defended each bunker, emplacement and sangar; but the combination of effective armoured, artillery and naval gunfire was too great. Most of the Argentinian artillery was also preoccupied with supporting 5 BIM on Tumbledown,

although the airborne gunners of GA Aerot 4, which had been supporting RI 7 all night, continued to do so. Some succour was given by Esc Exp Cl B 10 opening fire on the Scorpions and Scimitars, in the only armoured action of the entire campaign. A/RI 7, on the northern ridge, then gave way, and the defence collapsed. Esc Exp Cl B 10 counter-attacked dismounted, but failed, as did A/RI 3 from Reserva Z. RI 7 lost about 30 killed and a large number of wounded and missing in the two battles. The remnants retired in some disorder, and after the surrender on 14 June were assembled on Stanley Airport. Most were repatriated on the *Canberra*, although selected officers were retained until early July.

Regimiento de Infanteria 8

Regimiento de Infanteria 8 (RI 8) was, in 1982, a major component of Br I IX and based in Comodoro Rivadavia in southern Argentina. Its 800 all ranks were organised into three rifle companies, a headquarters and a service and support element; conscripts formed about 70 per cent of the unit, with varying degrees of military ability.

The regiment arrived on 5 April and established a garrison at Fox Bay, Sector URANIO (uranium). One platoon, 3/C/RI 8, was diverted to the Darwin Peninsula. A section also remained in Stanley and was absorbed into Agr Ej Malvinas Centro de Logistique as the regiment's B Echelon.

By 16 April the Fox Bay garrison, Fuerza Taaska Reconquistado, was reliant upon its own support weapons for artillery and air defence. The Command Post was established in the community centre, with rear link and teleprinter facilities supplied by Ca Comm 181. Medical facilities already existed in Fox Bay, and the regimental medical section was reinforced by a detachment from Ca San 9. Foot and heliborne patrols were frequent; but life at Fox Bay itself was relatively comfortable, with regular mail and

▲ *Two conscripts wash their clothes, possibly at Port Howard. The right hand wears Wellington boots and a field cap. The other wears a winter field cap with attached ear muffs and a civilian sweater. Both appear to be wearing tan overalls. The national insignia is again evident on the combat parka.*

▶ *A group of Marine Infantry, probably 5 BIM on Mt. Tumbledown, collect their pre-cooked meal from a container. A variety of headgear is evident including helmets, winter field caps and a wollen hat. Note that the hoods are integral to the combat jackets. The man walking away from the food container is wearing a one-piece overall, which was associated with the Marine Infantry. Note the soldier wearing a combat waistcoat, left centre.*

A conscript lies down behind a bipod-mounted 7.62mm MAG. Note the length of the belted ammunition. It would almost be impossible to carry this amount without it becoming awkward and cumbersome.

supplies. Relations with the inhabitants seems to have been adequate.

By mid-May British advanced forces had established OPs on East Falkland. Several air attacks on Fox Bay were experienced, on one occasion a Royal Navy Lynx helicopter being forced to take violent evasive action from sustained ground fire. On 16 May the Amphibious Support Force transport *Bahia Buen Suceso*, tied up alongside the jetty, suffered superficial damage during an air strike. Offshore shelling frequently set fire to stores dumps. Some cynics suggested that every unemployed Royal Navy ship had orders to harass the garrison.

In mid-May RI 8 had prepared plans to reinforce Goose Green by heliborne seizure of vital ground south of that point and an advance north to overrun the entire peninsula. Once secure, reinforcements from RI 5 would be brought over to consolidate the gains before striking out east towards Stanley.

After 21 May the British blockade in Falkland Sound began to have an effect as supplies ran short, not only for the garrison but also for the settlers. Sheep were therefore slaughtered and mined cows butchered. A heavy drop parachuted in ammunition, medical supplies and Wellington boots. The garrison was relatively unaffected by the fight for 'Bomb Alley', but on 26 May an attempt to land by a small group of British gunners from 148 (Meitakla) Bty RA was defeated. At the battle of Goose Green on 28 May the RI 8 platoon defending Boca House was overrun after putting up spirited resistance.

On 15 June an HMS *Avenger* landing party accepted the surrender of the Fox Bay garrison, the sick and wounded having previously been transferred to the hospital ship SS *Uganda*. The regiment was taken to the prison camp at Ajax Bay, from where most of the conscripts were repatriated within the week.

Recimiento de Infanteria 12

In 1982 Regimiento de Infanteria 12 (RI 12), with the honorary title 'General Arenales', was based in the northern province of Corrientes and was a major element of BrI III. Its 750 all ranks were a mix of conscripts who had only just completed their basic training, recalled reservists, and conscripts nearing the end of their national service. Many of the officers were new, and the CO had been in command barely three months.

In mid-April RI 12 was first deployed to defend the Atlantic seaboard and then given orders to transfer to the Chilean border. The unit was actually nearing the border when it received further orders for deployment to the Falkland Islands. On arrival in Stanley in mid-April, RI 12 first moved onto Two Sisters and Mt Harriet and then to Goose Green, leaving B/RI 12, Equipo Combate Solari, manning the Outer Defence Zone.

The Goose Green garrison was named Task Force Mercedes and consisted of C/RI 25, a platoon of RI 8, and Army and Air Force air defence. The airstrip was used by Pucaras and helicopters. Overall command lay with the Air Force commander while RI 12 assumed tactical command. At the beginning of May the garrison began to suffer from several air raids. On 15 May EC Guemes, drawn from C/RI 25, was despatched to man a patrol base at Port San Carlos. Four days later eight tons of stores were dropped by parachute to the garrison.

On 21 May the first direct contact with the British occurred when A/RI 12, manning the main defensive line across the peninsula, reported they were under attack by a battalion; in fact it was an SAS diversionary patrol covering the San Carlos landings. A day later A/GA Aerot 4 arrived with its four guns. Br I III then ordered A/RI 12 to deploy north of a minefield near Burnside House, unsettling the inexperienced troops.

Battle of Goose Green

Battle was imminent, and late on 27 May a section investigating movement at Camilla Creek House disappeared. Early on 28 May, A/RI 12 disintegrated in confusing night fighting with A/2 Para. Covered by a composite Servicio/RI 12, then manning the centre of the main defensive line, less than half of A/RI 12 reached the safety of Darwin Hill, already occupied by a C/RI 25 platoon. Heavy fighting developed as A/2 Para attempted, in vain, to capture the hill. About midday the RI 8 platoon at Boca House was overwhelmed by D/2 Para. A renewed British effort on Darwin Hill succeeded and the main defensive line collapsed. The EAM company, on the left flank, was quickly overwhelmed. A combined RI 12 and C/RI 25 force counter-attacked up the centre of the peninsula to relieve the pressure on the garrison, resulting in the 'white flag' incident, for which no one was to blame. The fighting became more violent.

On Mt Kent, EC Solari less one platoon were taken to Stanley Airport and then helicoptered to south of the settlement, but only about half managed to breach the British lines. The following morning RI 12, along with the remainder of the Goose Green garrison, surrendered. RI 12 lost 32 killed and about 70 wounded. Most of Task Force Mercedes were airlifted to Ajax Bay before being repatriated to Argentina on board the MV *Norland*. The missing EC Solari platoon was detached to RI 4 on Mt Harriet and was overwhelmed in the assault on that feature.

Regimiento de Infanteria 25

Regimiento de Infanteria 25 (RI 25) was, in 1982, an element of Br I XI, and based in Sarmiento in the central southern province of Chubut. At the time the regiment consisted of two rifle companies, a headquarters and service and support elements. Under the influence of Halcon 8, the regular cadre for Army commando units, Special Forces techniques were widely used. The regiment was unofficially named Regimiento de Infanteria Especial 25.

RI 25 were overjoyed to be selected for the Las Malvinas invasion, and a third rifle company was formed. On 2 April one C/RI 25 platoon was ferried ashore in the second wave by Ca Veh Anf/IM LARC-5s, cleared Stanley Airport and occupied the Yorke Bay Lighthouse. Two hours later the remainder of RI 25 was flown in and took up pre-planned positions around the Airport. A small parade was held to celebrate the recovery of the lost territories.

On 4 April C/RI 25 were flown to garrison the Darwin peninsula, where, contrary to the official policy of appeasement, a strict regime was imposed on the settlement. By 12 April C/RI 25 came under command of the FAA, then establishing an air base at Goose Green, reverting, in late April, to Army control when RI 12 arrived.

On 15 May a C/RI 25 platoon-sized grouping, Equipo Combate Guemes, established a patrol base at Port San Carlos. On 21 May its observation post on Fanning Head was abandoned, the retiring Argentinians extricating themselves from an SBS ambush. In Port San Carlos EC Guemes broke contact with 3 Para, shooting down two Gazelle helicopters and damaging a third. Some conscripts reached Stanley; others died in the attempt and a number were captured, suffering badly from the privations of weather and terrain.

During the battle of Goose Green a C/RI 25 platoon was ordered to assist A/RI 12, which had been shattered in the early hours of the battle by the leading 2 Para company breaching the main defensive line. They reached Darwin Hill, and for the next six hours doggedly defended the feature. Eventually it fell, shattering the main defence of the peninsula; only four conscripts rejoined C/IR 25. Meanwhile B I III, with responsibility for the Darwin peninsula, helicoptered about 50 EC Guemes survivors

A group of four Army conscripts outside their bunker on Stanley Common. Two wear temperate blouses while the others have donned the Argentinian Army Israeli-style quilted jacket. The soldier standing centre rear wears leather webbing and has an FAL slung over his shoulder. Two wear the winter cap, one with the muffs buttoned under his chin.

▲ A conscript poses in his weapon pit. The blue-white-blue national insignia is easily identifiable on his left sleeve.

► An unidentified lieutenant and a lieutenant-colonel pose outside a bunker, possibly their command post on Stanley Common.

to Goose Green. The two EAM companies then came under command of C/RI 25 as fighting developed around the schoolhouse. It decreased when three British personnel approached holding a white flag, and asked the astonished Argentinian defenders to surrender, which was turned down. The British returned to their lines, still carrying the white flag. A British GPMG gunner about 1,000 metres away and unaware of what was happening, but seeing Argentinian troops in the open, fired, wounding several conscripts. The Argentinians, furious at what they perceived to be a trick, shot the three British. The Paras, equally incensed and believing the Argentinians to have dishonoured the white flag of truce, attacked, and a violent battle developed around the schoolhouse, which was soon burning.

To the west, the two EAM companies collapsed and Task Force Mercedes was now in full retreat. C/RI 25 retired to high ground, where, supported by B/601 GADA GDF-002 Oerlikons firing in the ground role, they harried the advancing British; but by the onset of dusk, after 16 hours of fighting, the Argentinians were hemmed around Goose Green. The following morning the garrison capitulated. The nominal roll of C/RI 25 was short. One officer, four NCOs and eight conscripts lost their lives. An officer was awarded the Cruz La Nacion Argentina al Horacio Valor en Combate for rescuing a wounded NCO under fire.

In Stanley, RI 25 fretted, contemptuous of the British and the

conduct of the campaign. The constant bombardment of Stanley Airport had a demoralising effect on the regiment, and therefore it was with some satisfaction that RI 25 received the order to reinforce RI 7 on Wireless Ridge, but this and other moves never materialised. It was thus a bitter RI 25 that filed into captivity on 14 June; but, determined to maintain their pride, they marched in company columns into Stanley, for the first and last time, to be repatriated on the SS *Canberra*.

Compania de Commando 601

On 27 April 1982 Agr Ej Malvinas was reinforced with Compania de Commando 601 (Ca Cdo 601), an Army level Special Forces unit based in Buenos Aires. Its concept of operations was never really defined, and the unit of 15 officers and 50 NCOs evolved into a 'quick-reaction force' of a headquarters of six, a support element of eight, and three 15-man sections each consisting of two assault and one support squads.

The Army commandos initially carried out several familiarisation operations. Little of significance was found, although a 'kelper' suspected of passing information to the British Task Force was arrested in San Salvador settlement. Most of these operations were heliborne, although one patrol was embarked on a Prefectura Naval Argentina (PNA) cutter to carry out a recce of the coastline from Stanley to Cape McBride. Unfortunately a gale developed, and the following morning six very seasick and almost totally incapacitated commandos staggered off the cutter.

The unit also helped Ca PM 181 in several internal security operations, including cordoning a warehouse in which a resistance meeting was suspected. When the civilians filed out the next day it was established that they had merely been sheltering from air raids.

In mid-May a patrol cleared Port San Carlos ready for the insertion of EC Guemes. Two sections were also deployed to Pebble Island to assist in follow-up operations after the SAS raid. On 19 May two sections were flown to Port Howard to assist an RI 5 search for suspected British patrols. By 21 May, with the landing of the British at San Carlos, Ca Cdo 601 found itself split and in no position to react; however, the Port Howard patrols shot down a Harrier with a Blowpipe.

From 24 May for two days Ca Cdo 601 participated in the first combined Special Forces operation, designed to neutralise suspected enemy air defence screens in the Mt Usborn area, which included clearing Top Malo House. All patrols reported the 'going' difficult. Meanwhile attempts to recover the two stranded sections from West Falkland resulted in the loss of several Army helicopters.

On 28 May, all Special Forces were centralised for a major operation to establish a forward screen along Mt Estancia–Bluff Cove Peak–Smoko Mt, Ca Cdo 601 successfully establishing an OP on Mt Estancia. The newly arrived and untested Ca Cdo 602 was systematically destroyed while GOE were inserted into the Smoko Mt area. The operation was then cancelled when a Puma helicopter carrying a detachment from Ca FE 601 GN crashed on take-off, and the surviving patrols were ordered to return to Stanley. A Kawasaki 125cc motorcycle-mounted patrol was ambushed near Murrell Bridge on 31 May, and considerable efforts were made to recover the machines and the wounded. Ca Cdo 601 were then tasked to defend B Av C 601 operational base, and continued to assist Ca 181 PM. On 7 June a combined Ca Cdo 601 and Ca FE 601 GN patrol was ambushed near Murrell Bridge, but remained in the area all day, calling down artillery fire on enemy movement. On 14 June Ca Cdo 601 surrendered; most were repatriated, though some were retained until early July.

Compania de Commando 602

In mid-May Compania de Commando 602 (Ca Cdo 602) was raised, and arrived on 24 May, three days after the British had landed at San Carlos: 24 officers and 20 NCOs, all trained as Special Forces at some stage in their career, divided into three commando sections and headquarters.

On 28 May Ca Cdo 602 participated in the second Special Forces operation to harass and screen the British approaching from the west. Things went wrong from the very start. One section had the misfortune to be dropped in the middle of a British advanced forces position near Bluff Cove Peak and were systematically destroyed, losing most of their number, the survivors exfiltrating to Stanley.

The second section landed, as planned, near Top Malo House and then, in worsening weather, established an OP on Mt Simon. On hearing that the helicopter carrying the National Guardsmen had crashed, the OP was abandoned. After a most difficult march Top Malo House was reached; but unknown to them, a Royal Marines Mountain and Arctic Warfare patrol had reported their occupation of it to HQ 3rd Commando Brigade at San Carlos. The Section had a comfortable night, but soon after daybreak the timber building was stormed by a 19-man assault group from RM M & AW. The Argentinians responded and, covering each other, broke out of the burning building and took cover in a stream-bed. The fierce, close-quarter battle lasted about 30 minutes, during which the 12-man patrol lost two killed, six wounded and the remainder taken prisoner. The Royal Marines suffered two wounded.

The remnants of Ca Cdo 602 took part in several operations against the British, notably the forcing of an OP off Mt Wall and a fierce patrol battle at Murrell Bridge.

Compania de Fuerzas Especiales 601 de Gendarmerie Nacional

The 40-strong Compania de Fuerzas Especial 601 de Gendarmerie Nacional (Ca FE 601 GN) deployed to the Falkland Islands in mid-April. The Gendarmerie Nacional is a 12,000-strong force with a role to provide a frontier protection force, and thus its

Three cold officers, possibly from 3 GA, pose in front of a 4-wheel drive Mercedes. The captain does not wear any headgear, while the major, in the centre, wears a helmet. The right hand officer wears no rank.

Two conscripts pose with a 7.62mm MAG. Both wear temperate blouses. The gunner has a leaf pattern cover on his helmet. They may be C/RI 25 at Goose Green.

deployment was logical to Argentina's claim over the Falkland Islands.

On 28 May all Special Forces were centralised for an operation to establish a screen west of the Outer Defence Zone to observe and harass the British advance from San Carlos. The operation was beset with ill-luck from the very start and although Ca Cdo 601 has some success, the newly arrived Ca Cdo 602 underwent all sorts of problems that eventually led to the destruction of a section at Top Malo House. Disaster then overtook Ca FE 601 GN, when a B Av C 601 Puma crashed on take-off at the Racecourse killing two officers, four NCOs and gendarmes and injuring several others. This incident hastened the cancellation of the operation and orders were issued for the recovery of the surviving Special Forces. On 7 June a combined Ca FE 601 GN and Ca Cdo 601 patrol was ambushed near Murrell Bridge, but managed to extricate itself during some heavy fighting.

Interestingly, no Ca FE 601 GN prisoners were captured at the Argentinian surrender, and its participation in the campaign has only recently been acknowledged.

COMBAT SUPPORT

Air Defence

Air defence of the newly captured Malvinas was a priority, and within a few hours of the Royal Marine garrison's surrender Batallon de Antiaerea/Infanteria Marina (B A/IM) established a 13-battery Tigercat air defence complex around Stanley Airport and the town. Within the week a 12-gun single-barrelled 30mm

Hispano–Suiza battery had also been deployed. By mid-April the Centro de Informacion y Control (CIC) had been established to process all information on air defence through Grupo 2 VYCA, later designated as Escuadron 2 VYCA Malvinas. This FAA unit was equipped with AN/TPS-43 and AN/TPS-44 early warning radar, on high ground near Stanley Airport and later moved to western Stanley.

The FAA air defence consisted of Escuadron Antiaerea I and II, Grupo de Artilleria Antiaerea, equipped with the twin-barrelled 20mm Rheinmetal 202 (Rh 202) cannon, directed by the ELTA fire control concept, and a 12-gun single-barrelled 35mm GDF-001 Oerlikon battery connected to the Superfleder-maus air defence concept.

The Army Grupo de Aerea Defense 601 (GADA 601), with its attached elements from GADA 602, covered the south-west approaches. GADA 101 consisting of two batteries of twin-barrelled 35mm GDF-002 Oerlikons connected to a Skyguard fire control unit covered the northern approaches. In mid-April, 3/B/GADA 601, equipped with two GDF-002s and a Skyguard, was deployed to Goose Green, the air defences of which were enhanced later by the arrival of six FAA Rh-202s. B/GADA 101 with its eight Hispano–Suiza guns joined Ca Am 12.7/IM and 3/H/BIM 3 on Cortley Hill to protect fuel.

Army infantry units were reliant upon M2 0.50 Brownings for their air defence, although this was sometimes complemented by Blowpipe and SAM-7 Strela shoulder-launched missiles.

1 May was the first real test for the air defence, and although there was a series of mistakes and lack of co-ordination, the early-morning Vulcan raid and subsequent attacks by the Sea Harriers did allow for a shake-down period. A Sea Harrier did suffer from superficial damage. A damaged FAA Grupo 8 de Casa (G8C) Mirage III was accidentally shot down as it approached BAM Malvinas, killing the pilot.

Three days later GADA 601 claimed their first kill when the 3/B/GADA Skyguard shot down one of three Sea Harriers attacking BAM Condor. The same day an FAA G5C A-4B

Probably a platoon of C/RI 25 digging in at Fanning Head. Note the 'woodland' style covers of the steel helmets and the leather belt order.

Skyhawk, showing yellow identification panels, was also shot down, killing the pilot. As the British Task Force neared the Falkland Islands and the imminence of amphibious landings seemed likely, so British interdictions grew. RI 5 0.50 Brownings in the air defence role damaged a Sea Harrier, and a GR 3 Harrier suffered battle damage when it attacked a helicopter hide north of Mt Kent.

The landings at San Carlos on 21 May saw two 3 Commando Brigade Air Squadron Gazelle helicopters fall victim to ground fire from Argentinian troops withdrawing from Port San Carlos. Off Port Howard a GR 3 Harrier was shot down by a Blowpipe missile and the wounded pilot captured. During the battle for Goose Green one of two GR 3 Harriers, vectored to attack GA Aerot 4 M56 gun position, was shot down by 3/B/GADA 601 35mm Oerlikons. The FAA Rh 202 and Army 35mm guns also gave support in the ground role, but each was silenced in turn, the FAA guns when the airstrip was overrun and the Army weapons by an air-strike. Many of the British later spoke respectfully of the effectiveness of the air defence and the ground defence role.

On 30 May a GR 3 Harrier was damaged while strafing a column of troops (probably RI 4) withdrawing from Mt Wall to their main position on Mt Harriet and Two Sisters. A day later two more GR 3 Harriers suffered battle damage while making a low-level attack on BAM Malvinas. The Roland scored its only kill when, on 1 June, a missile struck a Sea Harrier, causing it to ditch; the pilot was rescued by a helicopter eight hours later. The battles for Stanley saw many close-support sorties by the Harriers and several suffered battle damage.

The GADA 2 detachment on Cortley Heights had meanwhile had a relatively quiet time until the early hours of 14 June, when a British advanced forces raid was repelled.

Grupo de Artilleria 3

Grupo de Artilleria 3 (GA 3) was the regimental artillery group of Br I III and based in Corrientes. The organisation was the four-gun battery, each equipped with the seven-crew Italian M56 105mm pack howitzer Oto Melara, nicknamed the Obus. Each battery had an artillery mechanic.

GA 3 deployed to the Falkland Islands on 17 April to support

Br I X, whose GA 10, with its US 105mm guns, was considered unsuitable for the Falklands. The Group was immediately placed on Stanley Common in support of the infantry regiments then arriving in response to the despatch of the British Task Force. Initially the guns were dug in, but with the approach of winter the gunpits soon filled with freezing water. Maintenance also became a constant battle. After 1 May the gun positions were regularly bombed and shelled. Ready-available ammunition became a problem, and the constant manning of the guns meant that little work could be done to repair the flooded gun-pits; consequently gun platforms were often unstable.

During the early June patrol battles around the Outer Defence Zone GA 3 disrupted British patrolling. When the Outer Defence Zone was assaulted on the night of 12 June, GA 3 provided rapid and accurate support and on more than one occasion held up British advances. Even after the zone had been breached and most of the Forward Observation Officers (FOOs) captured, GA 3 maintained accurate indirect fire on the captured features, making life very unpleasant for the occupying troops. This soon drew the attention of counter-battery fire and Harriers, the latter on more than one occasion 'toss-bombing' gun positions. GA 3 continued to support the defence of Stanley right up to the minute of surrender. On 12 June GA 3 took under command GA 101, with their Citefa 155mm howitzers, flown in that night and immediately brought into action.

When the surrender was announced the exhausted and filthy gunners were unable to spike their guns before being assembled and marched off to the Airport. GA 3 lost two gunners killed during the final battle for Stanley and another when a shell hit the Regimental Command Post. Most were repatriated on SS *Canberra* by 16 June.

Grupo de Artilleria Aereotransportado 4

Grupo de Artilleria Aereotransportado 4 (GA Aerot 4) supports the Brigada de Aereotransportado (Br Aerot) and is normally based at Cordoba. It has an airlanding and parachute role, and its personnel are entitled to wear the red beret and airborne wings. There were three four-gun batteries equipped with Italian M56 105mm pack howitzers.

GA Aerot 4, less its administrative elements, deployed to the Falkland Islands on 23 April, flying from its base in Cordoba, and was deployed onto Stanley Common in support of Br I III, which had lost its organic artillery group to Br I X. In early May A/GA Aerot 4 were deployed to Goose Green to support Task Force Mercedes. On 21 May two guns were loaded on board the Prefectura Naval Argentina (PNA) cutter *Rio Iguaza*, but after being attacked by two Sea Harriers in Choiseul Sound the captain beached his damaged vessel at Buttons Bay, where helicopters air-lifted the guns and their crews to Goose Green. One M56 had been badly damaged. The remaining two guns were flown in later.

A/GA Aerot 4 dug in behind A/RI 12, then covering the northern approaches to Darwin peninsula. The three guns registered, including on the night of 26 May, causing some momentary discomfort to 2 Para moving up to Camilla Creek House in preparation for the assault on the Darwin peninsula. The battery mechanic continued to work on the fourth gun.

During the battle for Goose Green the airborne gunners gave valuable support to the hard-pressed infantry and were only silenced with the inevitability of surrender. In the honoured tradition of gunners, the M56s were spiked to such an extent that all British efforts to repair them failed. The battery commander later said: 'We knew that 29 Commando Regiment had only recently given up the Oto Melaras for the Light Gun. Given half a chance they would repair the guns and use them against us.'

On Stanley Common the remaining two batteries were subjected to the stress of being a primary target for shelling and bombardment. They suffered flooding gun-pits, unstable gun platforms and irregular ammunition supply. Nevertheless, during the final stages of the battle for Stanley GA Aerot 4 provided accurate and timely support to the infantry, particularly during the battle for Wireless Ridge, and for the final counter-attack by A/RI 3.

Grupo de Artilleria 101

On 8 June Agr Ej Malvinas learnt that experiments to develop an airborne platform to transport an Argentinian Citefa L33 155mm howitzer, its crew and first-line ammunition of 140 rounds in a C-130 Hercules had been successful and that the first of four howitzers, from Grupo de Artilleria 101 (GA 101), could be expected to arrive by air. This was an unexpected bonus, as the British 105mm Light Gun outranged the M56. During the night of 12 June two howitzers were flown in and were immediately brought into action, shelling British positions on Mt Harriet, Two Sisters and beyond. The following night, as the battle for Mt Tumbledown raged, two more arrived, although unloading was disrupted by the enemy shelling BAM Malvinas and the threat of air attack. The two guns were too late to be brought into action and were captured the following day with their crews.

Cavalry

Escuadron de Exploracion Caballeria Blindada 181 (Esc Exp C Bl 181) was an Army-level armoured car unit, usually based in Buenos Aires. Equipped with 12 French-manufactured Panhard AML 90 four-wheeled armoured cars, with 90mm main armament, in near pristine condition and with very low mileages, it was deployed to the Falkland Islands on 7 April. It was soon joined by Escuadron de Exploracion Caballeria Blindada 10 (Esc Exp C Bl 10), the principal armoured recce unit of B I X, normally based in Buenos Aires; this unit was also equipped with Panhard AML 90s.

Marine Infantry, probably 5 BIM, queue for their food from a mobile kitchen. Judging by their dress and lack of combat parkas, it is probably a warm day in early winter.

Both units were initially assigned to Reserva Z to provide support for the Stanley, Fox Bay and Darwin peninsula sectors, a task that was to remain unchanged throughout the campaign. On 25 April orders were given to Ecs Exp C Bl 181 to establish a blocking position at Moody Brook covering the track to Estancia. On completion of the Reinforcement Phase, Esc Exp C Bl 10 again came under command of B I X, and two armoured cars were assigned to RI 3 and RI 6.

On the night of 13 June Esc Exp C Bl 181 provided dismounted reinforcements to 5 BIM, but were not used. During the battle for Wireless Ridge the squadron also engaged the Scimitars and Scorpions of the Blues & Royals, in the only armour-versus-armour engagement of the war. When Wireless Ridge was lost the dismounted Esc Exp C Bl 10 crews carried out an unsuccessful counter-attack against the feature. It was a near disaster, the unit suffering casualties soon after crossing the Start Line.

Both units surrendered with the remainder of the Argentinians and abandoned their armoured cars in Stanley, from where some were later taken back to the UK as trophies and others used as targets. When they were repatriated to Argentina both units were allowed to keep their guidons.

On 8 June a 100-strong detachment from the Regimiento de Grenaderos de General San Martin arrived with six 7.62mm MAGs; this unit is the horsed Presidential escort. On arrival it was detached to RI 1 'Los Patricios' and saw action on Mt Harriet, where 16 of its troopers were captured.

Communications

Agrupacion Ejercito Malvinas had its 50-strong integral signals unit, Compania de Communicacion 181 (Ca Comms 181). It was divided into a Seccion Radio Electronica (radio), Seccion Alambrica (line), Seccion Centro de Mesajes (COMCEM) and Seccion Servicio (service). For the duration of the campaign the Malvinas detachment was based in Stanley Post Office with a rear link to Bahia Blanco, its peacetime base. A network was established covering the three brigades. An Electronic Warfare detachment is known to have been present with Ca Comms 181, but left the islands in early June.

Two sappers pose beside a minefield sign.

Argentinian conscripts huddle against the rain, wind and snow on Mt Kent, therefore possibly men from RI 4. A heavy duty poncho gives some protection.

1: Sergeant, Ca Cdo Anf, Government House, 2 April

2: Rear-Admiral Carlos Büsser, Landing Force
   Commander, 2 April

3: Marine 2 BIM, Government House, 2 April

4: Marine Chaplain, Government House, 2 April

A

1: Infantry Private, April
2: NCO, Armoured Troops, April
3: Army Commando Company 601, May

B

1: Lt. Alfredo Astiz, South Georgia, late April
2: MAG gunner, RI 12, Goose Green, 28 May
3: Medic, 5 BIM, June

C

1: Marine, NCO N/5 BIM, Mt. Tumbledown, June
2: Brigadier Mario B. Menéndez
3: Lieutenant-Colonel Mohamed Ali Seineldin, RI25
4: MP, Ca PM 181, Stanley

D

Argentine leather equipment: see text for captions

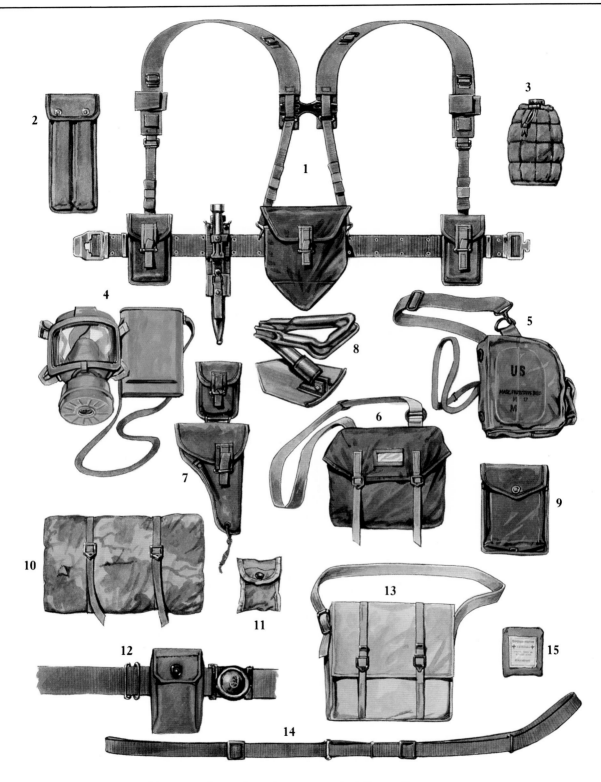

Tempex nylon web equipment: see text for captions

F

1: Brig.Gen. Luis Castellano, Commander IX Air Brigade
2: GOE Special Forces, Stanley Airport
3: FAA ground crew, Port Stanley
4: Helicopter pilot, B Av C 601

Field insignia: see text for captions

H

The Argentinian national sleeve insignia is clearly visible. The rifleman wears leather webbing. The soldier walking away wears a green nylon webbing yoke and waistbelt to which is fitted a leather ammo pouch, a sheathed bayonet and a low-slung nylon .45 pistol holster.

Each brigade had its integral signals unit, e.g. Compania de Communicacion 3 (Ca Comm 3) outside the Stanley environs, Compania de Communicacion 9 (Ca Comm 9) and Compania de Communicacion 10 (Ca Comm 10) in Stanley, each supporting its formation. Each was divided into the same three principal elements as Ca Comm 181, although Centro de Mesajes/Ca Comm 3 had teleprinter links from Stanley Post Office to Task Force Mercedes at Goose Green, RI 5 at Port Howard and RI 8 at Fox Bay. The radios used were Thompson-CSF HF sets, MEL's VRC 321 and 322 Clansman vehicle and manpacks, and US Harris Corp RF 3000, 3061 and 3062 HF sets.

Grupo de Ingenerios Malvinas

Landing with 2 BIM across the Yorke Bay beaches was the Army amphibious company, Compania de Ingenerios Anfibios 601 (Ca Ing Anf 601), who were detailed to breach any field defences and obstacles, lift mines and defuse booby-traps. In the event nothing was found. It was therefore with some relief that the sappers moved on to their next task—to clear Stanley Airport, ready for the fly-in of reinforcements.

Compania de Ingenerios Anfibios/Infanteria Marina (Ca Ing Anf/IM) also came ashore to begin preparing field defences and laying minefields for an extensive defensive network around Stanley and the Airport. A detachment was sent to Pebble Island, where it laid minefields, and built a command-detonated improvised explosive device that was fired with some effect during the SAS raid on 15 May.

Within the week Compania de Ingenerios 9 (Ca Ing 9), part of Br I IX, were despatched to Fox Bay, initially as garrison troops, until reinforced by RI 8 and RI 5 in Port Howard. At Goose Green, Ca Ing 9 sappers created a large minefield near the airstrip, which during the battle caused one 2 Para company to be deflected into the path of another company, causing some confusion.

By 15 April all engineers were regrouped under the title of Grupo de Ingenerios Malvinas (G Ing Malvinas). Ca Ing Anf/IM despatched sappers to RI 25 at the Airport and to BIM 5 on Mt Tumbledown and Mt William. The Marine sappers worked on the defence of the BAM Malvinas with only limited enthusiasm, but showed notable ingenuity in keeping the runway open after it had been struck by a single bomb during the 100 Squadron RAF Vulcan raid during the early morning of 1 May.

Ca Ing Anf 601 was tasked to assist RI 3 in building defensive obstacles around Mullet Creek. Compania de Ingenerios 10 (Ca Ing 10), part of Br I X, mined the Murrell Bridge and Hearndon Bay areas. By the end of May most of the principal field defences and mining tasks had been completed, although damage from the bombing and shelling throughout May would ensure continuous maintenance.

It is estimated that at least 12,000 mines were laid, the majority in defensive fields around Stanley. Some were laid on beaches where shifting sands concealed them; others sank in the peat, later to rise to the surface and become a threat to animals. In most instances minefields were wired off and demarcated with the word 'Mina' painted on a board, but the shelling and bombing often flattened the fences. Mistakes on their true location were made, although explicit instructions were issued that the records and plotting of minefields were to be carefully maintained. Some mines identified included the Argentinian plastic FMK 1 AP and FMK 3 AT mines, the Spanish plastic P4B AP and C3B AT, the Italian 8B33 AP and 8B81 AT, the Israeli box No 4 anti-booby trap and metallic No 6 AT, and US metallic M1 AT types.

As the British neared Stanley and began to probe the Argentinian Outer Defence Zone the sappers became involved in laying more mines, particularly in front of RI 4 on Two Sisters and Mt Harriet. During one such task a Ca Ing Anf/Im work party and its RI 4 protection became involved in a fierce firefight with a British patrol and suffered some casualties. A local truce was arranged with some engineers from 59 Independent Commando Squadron RE to recover the bodies. This marked the first direct contact between the Argentinian and British amphibious engineers.

When 3rd Commando Brigade assaulted the Outer Defence Zone only a small number of minefields had been plotted by the British; orders were given that the assaulting troops would have to run through any that were discovered, irrespective of the casualties. It was the detonation of a mine that alerted the Mt Longdon defenders to the approach of 3 Para. In the assault on Mt Harriet by 42 Commando (42 Cdo), the reinforced 1st Welsh Guards, tasked with securing the Start Line, misread a map and stumbled into a minefield, without detonating any but experiencing some difficulty in extricating the forward elements.

G Ing Malvinas detachments also seem to have performed very creditably as infantry. One Ca Ing 10 platoon helped defend the

A second lieutenant, possibly ADA/IM, poses beside a Tigercat SAM launcher. He wears a temperate blouse and trousers. On his waistbelt, just visible, is a low-slung holster.

eastern edges of Two Sisters, and on Mt Tumbledown Ca Ing Anf/IM played a key role, suffering 50 per cent casualties.

When the fighting was over many Argentinian sappers willingly gave their parole and assisted British engineers in charting minefields, lifting and identifying mines, dismantling and defusing booby-traps and other engineer tasks, including mending the Stanley filtration plant for desperately needed water.

Compania de Intelligencia 181

Little is known about the Argentinian Intelligence effort; suffice it to conclude that the April invasion forces were well prepared and had a good knowledge of likely British responses.

Campania de Intelligencia 181 (Ca Int 181) was the Army-level Intelligence detachment for Agrupacion de Ejercito Malvinas and was based in Government House. It had responsibility for the collection from a variety of sources and the collation and dissemination of information and intelligence. It is known that there were complaints about the lack of good current intelligence, but that was more because of the lack of information than incorrect assessments. There are several examples of reasonable basic intelligence on British units, ships and aircraft, likely landing methods and personalities—although the SAS were recorded as being based in Aldershot. Some interrogation of prisoners did occur, most of it unexpectedly civil, and therefore successful.

Batallon de Aviacion de Combate 601

Batallon de Aviacion de Combate 601 (B Av C 601) was part of the Commando de Aviacion del Ejercito, an element of the Infantry, and was based in Campo de Mayo, near Buenos Aires. It was organised into three companies. Compania de Helicopteros (Ca Heli/B Av C 601) was equipped with the Augusta A-109A, UH-1H Hirundo and SA-315B Lama, and had a protection and 'gunship' role. The troop-carrying capability was provided by Compania de Helicopteros Asalto A (Ca Aslt A/B Av

C 601) flying the SA-330L Puma and CH-47C Chinook, and Ca Aslt B/B Av C 601 with the Hirundo.

B Av C 601's first involvement in the capture of the Falkland Islands Dependencies was when Ca Aslt A/B Av C 601 deployed a Puma to support the scrap-metal merchants at Leith on South Georgia. It took part in the surveillance 'cat and mouse' with HMS *Endurance*, but on 3 April was shot down in the short battle for Grytviken while ferrying 1 BIM ashore.

B Av C 601 arrived on the Falklands on 6 April, some helicopters flying off ships, others being loaded into aircraft and re-assembled ashore. Eventually two Chinooks, three Augustas, five Pumas and nine Hirundos, with their attendant Compania de Aerea Maintaineros 601 (Ca Aereat 601), were in support of Agr Ej Malvinas, based at Moody Brook. Each aircraft had two pilots and a loadmaster, although the Hirundo co-pilots were eventually replaced by an engineer NCO. After the air raids of 1 May Argentinian helicopters were painted with a distinctive yellow recognition stripe.

In early May Ca Aslt B/B Av C 601 moved to a hide on Mt Kent, while the majority of Ca Aslt A/B AV C 601 flew to Goose Green. Both companies became involved in a variety of tasks including search and rescue, patrolling and supply delivery. Two Hirundos were converted to a Casevac role and painted white. Ca de Heli/B Av C 601 ranged island-wide to support the two assault helicopter units.

On 21 May Ca Aslt B/B Av C 601's hide was abandoned after a pre-emptive air raid. The following day an important mission by Ca Aslt A/B Av C 601 to fly ammunition to Port Howard had two Pumas out of three and one A-109A shot down by Sea Harriers. On 28 May Ca Aslt A/B Av C 601 abandoned its base at Goose Green when the peninsula was attacked and returned to Stanley; nevertheless, it flew at least two reinforcement missions in support of the beleaguered garrison.

After the surrender the British captured two Augustas, seven Hirundos (five of which were serviceable) and two Chinooks. Most were taken back to the United Kingdom.

Compania de Aerea Maintaineros 601

Compania de Aerea Maintaineros 601 (Ca Aereat 601) was the helicopter maintainence unit in support of Batallon de Aviacion de Combate 601 (B Av C 601). It began to arrive on 6 April and was deployed wherever the helicopters had their bases.

LOGISTIC SUPPORT

Centro de Logistique

As soon as the Falklands had been captured on 2 April, the supply of the garrison became a major feature of the Argentinian occupation, particularly during the Reinforcement Phase and also after the British landings. Initially chaotic, the logistic organisation began to take shape with the arrival of Brigada de Infanteria IX (Br I IX) and Br I X, both bringing their respective logistic elements, Batallon de Logistique IX (B Log IX) and Batallon de Logistique X (B Log X). These units set up their collection and distribution points in Falkland Islands Company (FIC) warehouses and buildings.

The Centro de Logistique, under command of G1/G4 at Agrupacion de Ejercito Malvinas, was then formed to co-ordinate all formation logistic matters. For onward transmission to the troops, each unit provided a small echelon for the collection and distribution of a wide variety of stores and equipment. In spite of the arrival of sufficient supplies from the mainland, Centro de Logistique never really solved the problems of keeping the front-line troops well fed, well clothed and healthy. The arrival of Br I III in late April, minus most of its heavy equipment (loaded onto a ship that never left Argentina), stretched resources to the limit.

All unit general service transport was centralised under G1/G4, and this soon led to complaints from units manning the Outer Defence Zone along Mt Wall–Two Sisters–Mt Longdon that essential stores were not arriving. The Unimog and Mercedes trucks has good cross-country capability, but few withstood the rigour of the rough terrain. Fuel was also precious, and this led to rationing. For units on East Falkland stationed outside Stanley the logistic plan collapsed. The road to the Darwin peninsula was appalling. Helicopters relieved the pressure somewhat, although the losses were severe.

The supply of West Falkland was slightly easier; Task Force shipping and requisitioned FIC vessels supplied the garrison at Port Howard, Fox Bay and Pebble Island; however, several vessels were sunk or damaged. Heavy parachute-drop supply was carried by C-130 Hercules to the garrison at Goose Green on 19 May and Fox Bay the following day. When the supply runs failed the Argentinian garrison resorted to the time-honoured method of requisitioning supplies, particularly fuel and food, generally in return for a requisition note or payment.

The flow of supplies from the mainland, which continued right up until the last night of the campaign, was regular and substantial, as proved by the immense amounts of food, rations, clothing, ammunition and equipment captured when Stanley fell.

Medical

All medical and dental units were drawn from the Cuerpo de Sanidad and were distinguished by Red Cross insignia on helmets and left upper arm brassards.

The first casualties sustained were during the invasion of 2 April, when the commander of the Compania de Anfibios Commando (Ca Anf Cdo) was fatally wounded and two others injured during the attack on Government House, all of whom were attended by a Marine Infantry corpsman. One 2 BIM conscript was slightly wounded when a B Veh Anf LTVP-7 came under fire during the advance through Stanley.

As the Argentinians consolidated, Br I IX and Br I X brought over their integral Compania de Sanidad IX (Ca San IX) and Compania de Sanidad X (Ca San X) respectively. Army-level surgeons and hospital staff supplemented these personnel, basing

An Army chaplain is flanked by a major on his right and a lieutenant-colonel on his left. The chaplain wears easily identifiable crosses on his helmet and combat jacket, ski-type gloves and black leather pads on his knees, presumably for kneeling on the damp ground in field services.

themselves in Stanley Hospital; a small hospital was also established in Port Howard. All units had at least one doctor with a small team of medics.

The cold, wet weather caused a considerable number of non-battle casualties, particularly amongst those units from the warmer climate of northern Argentina; trench foot, gastroenteritis and minor ailments such as colds were common. At the beginning of May the Argentinian garrison came under naval and air bombardment and the first battle casualties were sustained. Those that required evacuation were either put on board the hospital ship *Almirante Irizar* for further attention, or were flown back to Argentina. Some physchological casualties also began to appear, particularly in those units deployed in and around Stanley Airport.

Some dead were buried in Stanley cemetery, a simple cross marking the grave. Outside Stanley, the dead were buried either in settlement cemeteries or near where they died; these bodies were later exhumed and moved to the cemetery at Goose Green. Shortly after the war was over the shallow graves of two Special Forces soldiers were found overlooking San Carlos.

After Stanley surrendered, approximately 400 sick and wounded repatriated to Argentina on the *Almirante Irizar*. Medical personnel were retained under the terms of the Geneva Convention, although one doctor did attempt to smuggle a pistol on board the SS *Canberra* and lost his 'retained person' status.

Compania de Policia Militar 181

The only military police unit to be identified was Compania de Policia Militar 181 (CA PM 181), a 65-strong Army-level unit based in Buenos Aires.

▲ *Two FAA members pose on the runway at Stanley. The airman on the right wears dark blue cotton overalls with FAA rank epaulettes and a field cap. His companion sports the FAA insignia on his left breast and a multi-coloured civilian balaclava.*

◀ *A Marine Infantry officer is escorted by 40 Commando RM after being captured inside the San Carlos beachhead on 25 May. He wears a set of tan overalls secured by buttons. Note the Arran sweater with cable knitting.*

The unit landed very early on, and escorted some of the Royal Marine prisoners to Argentina. Its brief was to maintain law and order in conjunction with the civil police authorities and to maintain military discipline. Ca PM 181 was based in Stanley Police Station. Initially the unit also had a secondary role to provide infantry to units on Stanley Common. Ca PM 181 was involved in several incidents, including mounting the cordon around a Falkland Islands Company warehouse, where it was incorrectly suspected that a resistance meeting was being held. They were also involved in the arrest of several Falkland Islanders.

Incorporated into Ca PM 181 was a 40-strong dog unit complete with German Shepherd dogs. When these were captured the British wanted to keep the dogs, until it was realized they only understood Spanish!

A security detachment was attached to the military police, although its true affiliation is unclear. This unit was returned to Argentina in late April, apparently because of excessive zeal.

AIR FORCE

Grupo de Operaciones Especiales

Grupo de Operaciones Especiales (GOE) was formed in the early 1970s to support a perceived Fuerza Aerea Argentina (FAA) Special Forces capability, and operated with the helicopter-heavy VII Brigada Aerea at Base Aerea Militar MORN, outside Buenos Aires. The unit also has a parachute capability for military and search and rescue roles. The composition of GOE is not easy to assess, although about 40 men were taken prisoner when Stanley surrendered.

Equipo de Controle de Combate

Equipo de Controle de Combate (ECCO) evolved in the 1970s and was affiliated to 1 Brigada Aerea, the air transport formation of the FAA, based at BAM Palomar near Buenos Aires. Its role is to act as pathfinders for airborne operations. It also has a search and rescue capability, a useful asset given Argentina's interest in the Antarctic. ECCO is believed to be a small organisation with perhaps about 50 all ranks; a few were taken prisoner in Stanley.

Soon after the Argentinian invasion a Brigada de Aerotransportado 4 (Br Aerot 4) staff officer visited the Falkland Islands to discuss the feasibility of deploying airborne forces.

The use of aicraft quickly required the use of specialist FAA ground personnel, and GOE and ECCO found themselves on the Falklands. They were heavily involved in the Reinforcement Phase, during which over 9,000 troops and 5,000 tons of stores

Three members of EAM being searched at San Carlos on 30 May 1982 by the Intelligence Section HQ 3 Commando Brigade. All wear the standard Army field uniform and woollen hats. One was armed with a .45in.

Ballesto Molina pistol. These three had spent three days attempting to surrender but failed to attract the attention of British patrols. An 845 Naval Air Squadron Sea King eventually took them prisoner.

Vice Comodoro Wilson Pedrozo, who commanded the garrison at Goose Green, is greeted by Brigadier JHA Thompson, commanding 3 Commando Brigade, as he arrives at San Carlos after surrendering. He carries a holdall.

and equipment were flown in. The ground crews achieved a very quick turnround using the US disposable stressed platform, considerably easing the loading and unloading of aircraft. On 19 May eight tons of stores were parachuted to the Goose Green garrison, and the following day nine and a half tons at Fox Bay.

GOE seem to have done some helicopter patrolling with Escuadron de Helicopteros 7 COIN, the counter-insurgency unit also from 7 Brigada Aerea, and carried out an operation with Ca Cdo 601 on Mt Simon.

On 28 May GOE and Ca FE 601 NG participated in the Special Forces operation to harass British advances along the northern and southern approach routes, and operated in the Mt Usborn area. Further deployment was cancelled when the Puma helicopter carrying the National Guardsmen crashed, killing or injuring most of the occupants. GOE remained undetected and undisturbed, and eventually returned to Stanley. Following the capitulation of 14 June an observer noted the quiet demeanour of the FAA Special Forces, compared to the arrogance of the Army commandos and volatile Marine Infantry.

Escuala de Aviacion Militar

Although the Escuala de Aviacion Militar (EAM) was not a Special Forces unit, the activities of some of its personnel are worth mentioning.

On 14 April 1982 about 200 EAM officers and NCOs were despatched to the Falkland Islands. A 100-strong company was sent to Goose Green on airfield protection and subsequently took part in the battle, manning a defensive system down the eastern beaches of the Darwin peninsula, where it was quickly rolled up by 2 Para.

An unknown number of EAM units were detailed by Commando Fuerza Aerea Sud (Cdo FAS), the FAA organisation controlling air operations around the Falklands, to form self-sufficient teams of about five men to man radars and beacons. The distrust between the FAA and CANA resulted in some patrols being complemented by Navy Special Forces. The British continued to conduct sweeps, and in one small engagement two Argentinians were killed, their bodies later being found in shallow graves.

The surrender of Task Force Mercedes meant that many of the surviving patrols found themselves cut off. Some teams reached Stanley, undergoing intense privations as they trekked eastwards; others were never heard of again. One team spent three days trying to surrender, but none of the British patrols they saw seemed interested; eventually a Sea King 'Jungly' crew took them prisoner. They were probably the most grateful prisoners the British captured during the campaign.

Unit	Officers	NCOs	Conscripts and equivalent	Unit	Officers	NCOs	Conscripts and equivalent
1 BIM			2	B Log 3		1	
5 BIM		2	15	Ca San 3		1	1
B/B A Cam/IM			2	Cdo/Br I X			2
Ca AMT 12.7/IM			7	Esc Bl C 10		3	3
B AA/IM			2	B Log 10		2	
Ca Ing/IM		1	3	Ca Comm 10			1
				Ca Ing 10			2
RI 1			1	GADA 601	1	1	4
RI 3			5	B Av C 601	3	3	
RI 4	2	4	17	B Log Con 601	1		
RI 5			8	Ca FE 601 GN	2	4	1
RI 6		2	10	Ca Cdo 602	2	3	
RI 7	1	2	33	B/GADA 101		1	2
RI 8		1	4	Esc Expl C Bl 181	1		
RI 12		4	31	B Comm 181			1
RI 25	1	4	8	Agr Ej Malvinas		1	1
GA 3	1	1		FAA Malvinas	1	8	5
GA AT 4			3				
Cdo/Br I III			4		16	49	178

THE PLATES

Research & Commentary by Paul Hannon

The national arms industry was well developed in Argentina prior to the 1982 conflict. The state arsenals produced everything from bullet to tanks, and arms production was an important source of foreign currency. Alongside this armament production a flourishing clothing and equipment industry had emerged and the vast bulk of material used in the Falklands was Argentine produced. This material was often of poor quality however and was never available in the amounts required by a sizable proportion of the units deployed to the islands. Veterans of the conflict remain very bitter about their treatment by officers and regular NCOs, whose concern for their own personal comfort often took precedence over tactical considerations or the welfare of their troops.

The supply system was equally disorganised and chaotic, witness the large amounts of unissued new clothing and large stocks of food that were discovered after the Argentine surrender. Mixed with the indigenous Argentine equipment were examples of old US-supplied equipment along with isolated examples from NATO and other sources. Where these have been identified they have been noted in the following plates captions.

Insignia, apart from rank badges, do not appear to have been worn by the majority of units involved, and where used seem to have been confined to NCOs.

Body armour was again not worn to any great extent and the few captured examples, usually 50s US issue or current commercial patterns, were probably acquired on an individual basis. Protective Anti-Gas equipment was employed in a similarly haphazard way. The Army issue gas-mask was the US M17 type, although other older styles were also issued; none appear to have been carried in the field.

The description US M1 helmet is used throughout the captions for simplicity. A number of helmets were of US origin but many had been relined by the Argentines and a proportion of the steel shells were also Argentine produced. The majority of helmets were therefore of inferior construction and materials and most seem to have been in a poor state of repair.

A1: Sergeant, Ca Cdo Anf; Government House, 2 April
In a classic image of the capture of NP 8901 at Government House, this NCO was seen in a series of photographs of the rounding up of the Royal Marine garrison. He wears uniform and equipment typical of Ca Cdo Anf, and was later identified as Sgt I. M. Batista. He wears the Marine and Naval issue one-piece overall in olive green. This has a fly-fronted full-length buttoned opening, a drawstring waist and ankles, and a field dressing pocket on the upper left sleeve. On each leg is a small cargo pocket. Over this he wears a quilted sleeveless body warmer, and windproof gauntlets with reinforced palms. His equipment consists of an Argentine Tempex web belt which has a US-style quick-release buckle, and an unusual shoulder yoke similar to the US M56 pattern.

At his right hip is a holstered 9mm Browning Hi-Power pistol, and just visible on the left side are twin tan-coloured leather ammo pouches for his silenced L34A1 Sterling sub-machine gun. Considerable latitude seems to be allowed in the choice of weapons; amongst those seen were L2A3 Sterlings, both versions of the standard Argentine FN, PA3 sub-machine guns, and in one or two instances Uzis. Rucksacks similar to US Vietnam tropical issue were utilised.

Headgear in the assault was a simple black woollen comforter. Ca Cdo Anf are thought to wear a black beret with a white metal version of the company crest (see Plate H). Some were seen to don brown or khaki berets with an unidentified circular badge surmounted by a naval coronet. Also seen was a semi-circular sand-coloured disc. These may have been worn by the 12 men of the Buzo Tactico team mistakenly credited with the capture of Government House.

A2: Rear-Admiral Carlos Büsser, Landing Force Commander; 2 April

Photographed soon after the British surrender, Admiral Büsser wears the camouflage uniform first introduced around 1980. The particular jacket worn here is of a later type, seemingly influenced by US BDU-style fatigues. It lacks the epaulettes and exposed buttons seen on earlier issue, and all closures and pockets, which are of the bellows type, are fitted with velcro. The matching trousers have large cargo pockets on each leg.

Camouflage clothing appears to have been largely limited to dedicated Special Forces units or those with a specialist function. Examples with both Naval and FAA markings have been noted. It does not appear to have been widely used by Army units with the exception of Ca Cdo 601 and 602.

Büsser wears the Marine pattern camouflage cap with its distinctive chrome ventilators. Rank insignia of a single gilt star is

Showing the difficult conditions in which the Army and Marine gunners had to operate: the gun is an Italian Oto Melara 105mm pack howitzer, which is conventionally crewed by eight gunners, *has a range of 10,570 metres. The position is waterlogged because of the rain and the high water table around Stanley. The gunpit appears to be covered by a very small, sparse camouflage net.*

pinned through both lapels and the cap. An olive green scarf is also worn.

A3: Marine 2 BIM; Government House, 2 April

This member of the 900-strong invasion force wears the distinctive brown temperate version of the Marine service dress; a heavier winter-weight uniform with a quilted lining also exists. Note the yoking at the shoulders and the shaped pocket flaps. He is equipped with an older pattern of webbing ammo pouches with a 'lift the dot' type closure, and web belt with bronzed clasp complete with the Marine crest. The rifle is an Argentine-manufactured FN FAL 50.61 folding-stock SLR. The helmet is the US M1 with an Argentine pattern helmet cover.

A Royal Marine of NP 8901 observed that this battalion effected a very theatrical air, festooned with ammunition and equipment and with helmet chin straps swaying, although they had taken little part in the fighting.

A4: Marine Chaplain; Government House, 2 April

With a heavily bandaged head wound, this padre conducts a service at the flag-raising ceremony on the morning of the invasion. He wears an olive green winter version of the Marine/Naval service dress. Note the crucifix on the front of his steel helmet, and the Red Cross brassard on his left arm.

B1: Infantry Private, April

This newly arrived reinforcement is clothed and equipped in a style typical of the majority of the Army garrison. He wears a US M1 steel helmet with an olive green cover made from a combat

jacket hood. Under the helmet he wears a fur pile winter cap. The padded parka is a commercially produced version of the Dubon, made under contract in Israel. He wears standard green Army fatigue uniform, and black leather high boots of Army pattern. He has a folding stock FN 50.61, made under license at Rosario in Argentina. His web belt and pouches are of the Argentine-manufactured Tempex type, to which he has attached a Spanish M5 hand grenade. He is carrying a green nylon kit bag and rolled sleeping mat.

B2: NCO, Armoured Troops, April
Armoured troops wore the black beret, here with the insignia of Esc Exp C Bl 181. A rank insignia tab is buttoned to the tunic pocket. He wears a Tempex waistbelt with a US black leather pistol holster.

B3: Army Commando Company 601, May
This member of Ca Cdo 601 wears the first pattern of camouflage fatigues, which are identified by the exposed buttons on all pockets and simple cargo pockets on the legs. Over this is worn one of several types of combat vest, in this case with magazine pouches on each side of the upper chest. Two M67 grenades are held in small pockets. This style of vest has a detachable cargo pack at the rear. He wears the Army Commando's beret of coarse green woollen cloth, with an enamel badge (see Plate H). His web equipment is the Tempex waistbelt with a holstered 9mm Browning. Note his 'polo-neck sweater' chest warmer, and Marine issue boots. He is armed with FAL 50.63 folding-stock rifle.

C1: Lt Alfredo Astiz; South Georgia, late April
Commanding a mixed detachment of 14 sailors and Marines, the infamous Astiz wore Marine camouflage uniform with red on blue slip-on ranking (*Teniente de Navio*) attached to the shoulder straps. Standard fur pile winter caps were worn, in the olive green colour. He was armed with a Browning pistol and carried an FAL 50.63 rifle. Note the Marine issue boots, recognisable by the mixture of eyelets and hooks and the heavy duty soles.

C2: MAG gunner, RI 12: Goose Green, 28 May
In common with other Argentine infantry units the rifle platoon (*seccion tiradores*) consists of 44 men commanded by a lieutenant or captain, in three rifle sections (*grupos tiradores*) and a support weapons section. A rifle section is in turn subdivided into two *equipos* each commanded by a junior NCO. The 12-man support weapons section has two FN MAG machine guns, each crewed by two men, which are usually mounted on lightweight tripods. This MAG gunner wears standard green fatigues Israeli type parka, and knitted woollen hat, and a standard Tempex web belt on which he carries two Spanish M5 grenades and a US compass pouch. He is draped with copious amounts of 7.62mm ammunition. Just visible is a holstered Browning pistol.

C3: Medic, 5 BIM; June
Medical personnel wore the red cross on a white disc or square painted (or sometimes stitched) onto the helmet cover. A simple red cross brassard is worn on the upper left sleeve. The medical bag is a Marine infantry haversack with a painted red cross insignia. He holds a field dressing in its distinctive blue plastic cover. He wears a winter-pattern combat jacket, much longer than the standard pattern. This is lined, with a full-length zippered front and has a permanently attached hood.

An Argentinian Army conscript stands outside a bunker. He carries a slung FAL. Note the second magazine taped to the one fitted to his rifle. The rounds can clearly be seen. His webbing is leather.

D1: Marine NCO N/5 BIM; Mt Tumbledown, June
This well-equipped NCO wears an unusual combat vest, possibly unique to this unit. The large front pockets each hold one magazine for his folding-stock FAL. A dressing pocket is located on the upper left chest. The vest has an integral pistol holster, which in this instance contains a .45 Model 1927 automatic or a Ballester Molina. Note the twin pistol magazine pouches on the lower left. This Marine has tied a cord around his waist from which are hung two M67 series grenades. Under the vest he wears the one-piece Marine issue overall (see A1) with his rank insignia pinned to each collar. He has a pair of US-style goggles strapped around his upper left arm, ready for use; these widely issued items had been acquired from various sources—US, French and possibly Israeli. His helmet is a US M1 with

◄ *A file of defeated Argentinian troops move into Stanley along Ross Street sometime during 14 June.*

▼ *Argentinian Air Force await repatriation from Stanley on 19 June after being held at the Airport since 15 June. The identification of the unit is not known. The officer appears to be wearing the wool lined trousers. One in the front rank wears Wellington boots.*

MlC parachutist's liner and web chinstrap. The helmed cover is of Argentine pattern camouflage material and has a foliage band cut from a rubber innertube. Note the camouflage kerchief in US 'duck hunter'-style pattern.

D2: Brigadier Mario B. Menéndez
Governor and Commander in Chief Malvinas, Menéndez wears standard Army pattern olive green fatigues, the collar points bearing the bullion leaf insignia of a general officer. Over this he wears a superior quality padded jacket used by some senior officers of the garrison, and also issued to Special Forces units. He wears issue brushed cotton gloves, which are wool lined, in a light tan colour. He carries a general's silver-topped baton.

D3: Lieutenant-Colonel Mohamed Ali Seineldin, RI 25
Along with the other members of his 'Regimiento Especial' Seineldin wore the Israeli-made parka and olive green fatigues. The unusual configuration of their equipment, however, deserves mention. Some wore Argentine waistbelts but the majority appear to have worn US M56 or M67 nylon waistbelts, with the yoke from the ALICE equipment. Standard green leather FAL pouches were retained. Seineldin follows this pattern and in addition has an archaic-looking mapcase similar to WWI types. His binoculars are of a similarly elderly style with a protective eye-piece cover. His rank is indicated by a chest-tab. He has two M67 grenades attached to his equipment yoke. The Argentine-manufactured walkie-talkie was of poor quality and range, but was widely used. The green velvet beret, worn by all ranks, has the crossed rifles badge surmounted by the number '25' worked in bullion thread; Other Ranks wore the crossed rifles only. Unusually this unit adopted the US leaf pattern helmet cover for wear by all ranks. Further distinctive features were the national tricolor worn on the upper sleeve of the parka, and the company patches worn (see Plate H).

A group of Marine Infantry, probably 5 BIM on either Tumbledown Mt or Mt William, pose for a photograph before or after a meal, judging by the mess tins held by some. Several wear helmets covered with the 'woodland' pattern cover; *others wear the classic Marine Infantry field cap, although one, front left, sports a woollen balaclava. Second from right in standing group of four wears a battle waistcoat.*

D4: MP Ca PM 181; Stanley
He wears olive green fatigues with a PM brassard on the left sleeve. A white leather belt was worn, and a white lanyard at the right shoulder, the latter presumably for a whistle. Two schemes of helmet insignia have been noted: the letters 'PM' stencilled in white on an olive green helmet, and a white-painted liner with black stencilling as illustrated here. At least one MP was photographed wearing black leather jackboots.

E: Argentine leather equipment
(1) Green leather infantry equipment consisted of waistbelt, pouches (each holding two FAL magazines), FAL type A knife-bayonet with leather frog, old aluminium water bottle with canvas cover, yoke and brace attachments.
(2) German-style entrenching tool and cover.
(3) US type folding shovel and cover.
(4) German-inspired felt-covered water bottle; some of these were later converted with a nylon neck and plastic screw cap.
(5) Rolled poncho and shelter quarter in leather cargo straps.
(6) Model 1909 sidearm in leather frog.
(7) Leather holster for .45 cal. pistols.
(8) Twin pistol magazine belt pouch.
(9) Twin pouch for PAM 2 sub-machine gun magazines.
(10) Rifle cleaning kit and contents in leather belt pouch.
(11) Belgian-made rifle-grenade sight case.

(12) First field dressing in plastic cover.
(13) Map case in brown leather.
(14) Leather holster for 9mm pistols, with integral ammo pouch, leg ties and supporting straps.
(15) Officer's sword belt.
(16) Green leather rifle sling.

F: Tempex nylon web equipment:

(1) Nylon infantry equipment consisted of an eyeletted waistbelt with US-style quick-release buckle, a nylon version of the FAL pouches, an FAL Type C bayonet for the folding-stock rifle, shoulder yoke in nylon and black plastic—in this case an 'H' configuration, but a 'Y' version has also been noted; and a nylon cover for the Tempex copy of the US folding E-tool.

(2) Nylon version of the sub-machine gun ammo pouch.

A file of FAA prisoners. Of interest is that the combat trousers and jacket appear to be lined, probably with thick wool. Trousers lined with wool were later recovered from captured clothing stocks. These men may have been involved in airfield dispersal duties.

(3) Plastic moulded water bottle in a quilted nylon cover.
(4) Finnish-made gas mask and container used by FAA units.
(5) US M17 gas masks used by Army units.
(6) Nylon 'butt pack' haversack.
(7) Nylon compass/pistol magazine pouch.
(8) Argentine copy of US folding E-tool.
(9) Nylon rifle cleaning kit pouch.
(10) Nylon cargo straps with folded US leaf pattern shelter quarter.
(11) US compass pouch.
(12) Marine old-style web pouches and waistbelt. These were sometimes worn in conjunction with WWII US Marine Corps suspenders and M14 pouches.
(13) Marine issue haversack in green canvas.
(14) Nylon rifle sling.
(15) First field dressing.

G1: Brigadier-General Luis Castellano, Commander, IX Air Brigade

Seen here during the hours following the invasion, Castellano wears the late issue olive green fatigues. These lack the exposed

buttons of earlier issues, having concealed buttons at the chest and press stud closures on the pockets. He wears the blue-grey SD cap of an FAA general officer, with national cockade, gilt fittings and braided peak. Ranking, a shoulder slide, is attached to the left pocket front; in the case of FAA officers this was dark blue on blue-grey. The qualification badge of an FAA senior pilot is worn pinned above the left pocket. He wears a Sam Browne belt, and an open-topped pistol holster with diagonal supporting strap is worn at the left hip. All leather equipment worn by FAA units is issued in bright tan finish.

G2: GOE Special Forces; Stanley Airport
This member of the 40-strong GOE contingent wore the latest issue one-piece camouflage overall. All openings and bellow pockets had velcro fastening. It is issued with a cloth waistbelt but this is often removed. Examples of these suits with both FAA and Marine markings have been noted. GOE members wear a dark blue beret with a shield-shaped enamel badge (see plate H). He wears Tempex nylon LBE with twin nylon pouches for his PA3 sub-machine gun. Footwear consists of FAA black leather boots. A member of NP 8901 has commented on the reserved and

efficient demeanour of the members of this unit, with whom he came in contact at Stanley Airport.

The similarly dressed and equipped ECCO air transport formation (see text) wore a turquoise beret with their insignia of a parachute and payload; these berets were noted to have faded to a greyish-pink colour.

G3: FAA ground crew, Port Stanley
Photographed after the surrender, this airman wore FAA issue fleece-lined jacket and trousers. These olive green jackets have a fly-front, and concealed press stud closure on all pockets. They are lined with white wool pile material and have a similarly lined integral hood. This *Cabo* (senior aircraftsman) wears in addition a quilted nylon jacket liner and issue heavy sweater. He has attached a pair of goggles to his fur pile cap. These caps, seen

A group of Army conscript prisoners in Stanley. Those in the foreground wear the Israeli-style winter combat jacket. The soldier in the centre rear (with an unsecured epaulette) appears to be wearing a temperate combat jacket.

◀ *The commanding officer of 3rd Infantry Regiment, Tte. Col. David Comini (right) and an unidentified Major seen here outside the British Antarctic Survey office in Port Stanley after the surrender. They had both been selected for further interrogation. They wear the Israeli manufactured parka with rank tabs suspended from a small button on the upper left chest. Note the national cockade (blue/white/blue) pinned to Comini's Argentine made winter cap.*

▼ *Special category prisoners are assembled outside the British Antarctic Survey offices. This group includes FAA with lined trousers and jackets, medics, Marines, Army and Coastguard.*

throughout the garrison, had been obtained from various sources; amongst those noted were Bundeswehr issue, Argentine-made examples (distinguished by their large baseball cap peaks), and even Korean War vintage US examples complete with original labels. They were supplemented by an astonishing variety of knitted woollen cap comforters and scarves. He wears a pair of heavy soled thermal boots. Green brushed cotton-lined gloves were also issued.

G4: Helicopter pilot, B Av C 601

This Augusta pilot is wearing the standard flying equipment issued to all Army aircrew. He wears an M1A1 flight jacket with the battalion insignia on the upper right sleeve. His flight suit is the US CWU-27 model, although Argentine copies of both the suit and the flight jacket exist. West German flight overalls have also been noted. The helmet is the US SPH-4C version. Green FAA issue gloves were often worn.

Plate H: Field insignia:

(1) Sleeve patch, Amphibious Commando Group.
(2) Woven patch on pin-back leather disc, thought to be recognition device.

A happy column of Marine Infantry, probably from Pebble Island, photographed at Ajax Bay sometime after 15 June.

The man at right front wears a new style camouflaged jacket with deep pockets.

(3) Sleeve patch of 2nd Marine Infantry Battalion, printed on plastic.
(4) 25th Infantry Regiment beret badge, worn on green velvet beret.
(5) Sleeve patch of RI 25, specially designed for Malvinas operation.
(6) Rank tab worn on Army and Marine uniforms and parkas; red vinyl on olive green uniform cloth.
(7) Army Commando beret badge.
(8) FAA rank chevron worn above left pocket by Other Ranks.
(9) Marine beret badge.
(10) Sleeve patch, 1st Marine AA Battery; moulded plastic.
(11) GOE beret badge.
(12) ECCO beret badge.
(13) Subdued OR's parachute wing.

Notes sur les planches en couleur

A1 Combinaison réglementaire vert olive d'une pièce pour la Marine et les Forces navales. Il porte au-dessus un gilet matelassé sans manche et des gants protégeant du vent dont les paumes sont renforcées. Ceinturon argentin en toile Tempex, pistolet Hi-Power Browning de 9 mm sure la hanche droite; sacs doubles à munitions en cuir fauve portés sur la gauche; mitraillette Sterling avec silencieux. Pour coiffure un simple cache-nez en laine noir. A2 Cet uniforme de camouflage a été introduit vers 1980; Modèle de képi de camouflage de la marine avec aérations distinctives en chrome. L'insigne de rang est épinglé sur les deux revers et sur le képi; il porte également une écharpe vert olive. A3 Tenue de service brune pour climat tempéré.

Farbtafeln

A1 Einteiliger, olivgrüner Overall für Marine und Marineinfanterie. Trägt darüber wattierte, ärmellose Weste und windfeste Handschuhe mit verstärkten Handflächen. Argentinische Stoffkoppel, 9mm Browning Hi-Power an rechter Hüfte; zwei braune Leder-Munitionstaschen links; Sterling-Maschinenpistole mit Schalldämpfer. Kopfbedeckung ist ein einfaches schwarzes Wolltuch. A2 Tarnuniform seit etwa 1980; Marineinfanterie-Tarnmütze mit typischen Chrom-Luftschlitzen. Rangabzeichen an beiden Aufschlägen und auf Mütze; olivgrünes Halstuch. A3 Braune Marineinfanteri-Uniform für gemäßigtes Klima; Munitionstaschen älteren Datums, Koppel mit Bronzeschnalle und Marineinfanterieabzeichen. Gewehr FN

Modèles plus anciens de sacs de munitions et ceinturon en toile avec boucle de bronze et écusson de la Marine. FN FAL SLR fabriqué en Argentine. Casque US M1 et housse argentinienne. A4 Version d'hiver vert olive de la tenue de service pour la Marine/les Forces navales. Notez le crucifix sur l'avant du casque en acier et le brassard au Croix Rouge sur le bras gauche.

B1 Casque en acier US M1 avec housse vert olive confectionnée dans un capuchonde veste de combat, et lunettes. Calot d'hiver avec fourrure sous le casque. Version commerciale de fabrication israélienne de parka Dubon matelassée. Treillis réglementaire de l'Armée vert, bottes hautes en cuir noir, monture de fusil pliante FN 50.61. Ceinturon en toile Tempex fabriqué en Argentine, grenade à main, espagnole, M5, vert en nylon pour kit, matelassage roulé. B2 Béret noir avec insigne Esc Exp CBL 181. Plaque d'insigne de range boutonné sur la poche de la tunique, ceinturon Tempex avec étui de pistolet en cuir noir. B3 Premier modèle de treillis de camouflage, veste de combat avec sacs pour chargeurs sur la partie supérieure de la poitrine, deux grenades M67 dans les petites poches. Béret en laine vert de commando militaire avec écusson en émail. Equipement en toile Tempex avec Browning de 9 mm dans l'étui, gilet de type "pull à col roulé" et bottes réglementaires de la Marine. Il est armé d'un fusil à monture repliable FAL 50.63.

C1 Uniforme de camouflage de la Marine avec insigne de rang rouge sur fond bleu à passants sur les pattes d'épaule. Béret d'hiver en fourrure vert olive, pistolet Browning, fusil 50.63 FAL et bottes réglementaires de la Marine. C2 Cet artilleur MAG porte un treillis standard vert, un chapeau de laine tricoté et un ceinturon en toile Tempex. Deux grenades espagnoles M5 et une poche pour compas US. Enroulées autour du corps des munitions de 7,62 mm et pistolet Browning dans un étui. C3 Insigne médical sur la housse du casque, simple brassard à croix rouge sur la partie supérieure de la manche gauche. La trousse médicale est une musette de l'infanterie de la Marine avec croix rouge peinte sur l'insigne. Paquet individuel de pansement sous protection plastique bleue et veste de combat, modèle d'hiver.

D1 Veste de combat peu courante avec grandes poches devant, poche pour paquet individuel de pansement à gauche sur la partie supérieure de la poitrine, étui intégral à pistolet. Notez les poches doubles pour chargeurs de pistolet sur la partie inférieure à gauche. Deux grenades, série M67 avec cordon autour de la taille, une combinaison réglementaire d'une pièce de la Marine avec insigne de rang épinglé sur chaque col. Lunettes de style US, casque US M1 et housse de modèle argentin avec bande de feuillage déboutonné dans une chambre à air en caoutchouc. Notez le mouchoir de style "chasseur de canard" US. D2 Treillis standard militaire vert olive avec insigne doré en forme de feuille d'un général sur les pointes du col. Il porte au-dessus une veste rembourrée de qualité supérieure, des gants en coton gratté, fourrés en laine et un baton de général d'dessus argenté. D3 Parka de confection israélienne, treillis vert olive, étui de carte d'aspect archaïque et jumelles. Le rang est indiqué par la plaque de poitrine; deux grenades M67 sont attachées à l'empiècement de l'équipement; walkie-talkie fabriqué en Argentine. Béret en velours vert, écusson aux fusils croisés et le chiffre "25" en fil torsadé. D4 Treillis vert olive, brassard PM sur la manche gauche, doublure de casque peinte en blanc et au pochoir en noir.

E1 Equipement d'infanterie en cuir vert; ceinturon, poches, baïonnette-couteau A type FAL avec bélière en cuir, ancien bidon à eau en aluminium avec étui en toile, empiècement et fixations de bretelles. E3 Pelle plainte et housse de type US. E4 Bidon à eau avec étui en feutre. E5 Poncho roulé et quart de tente dans des courroies de cuir de chargement. E6 Petite arme, un modèle de 1909, dans la bélière en cuir. E7 Etui en cuir pour pistolet de calibre .45. E8 Poche double sur le ceinturon pour chargeurs de pistolet. E9 Poches doubles pour chargeurs de mitraillette. E10 Kit de nettoyage du fusil dans la poche du ceinturon. E11 Etui de visée de grenade pour fusil lance-grenade. E12 Paquet de pansement individuel sous protection plastique. E13 Etui de carte en cuir brun. E14 Etui en cuir pour pistolet de 9 mm. E15 Bélière d'officier. E16 Bandoulière de fusil en cuir.

F1 Equipement en nylon d'infanterie avec poches FAL en nylon, une baïonnette C, type FAL, une housse en nylon pour la version Tempex de l'outil pliable E US. F2 Poche en nylon pour munitions de mitraillette. F3 Bidon à eau en plastique dans une housse matelassée en nylon. F4 Masque à gaz et coffret. F5 Masque à gaz US M17. F6 Musette en nylon "de paquetage pour butte". F7 Compas en nylon/sac de chargeurs de pistolet. F8 Copie argentine de l'outil pliable US E. F9 Poche en nylon pour kit de nettoyage de fusil. F10 Sangles de chargement en nylon; quart de tente à motif feuillu US. F11 Poche pour compas US. F12 Modèle ancien de poches de toile de la Marine et ceinturon. F13 Musette réglementaire de la Marine. F14 Bandoulière de fusil en nylon. F15 Paquet de pansement individuel.

G1 Treillis vert olive datant de la dernière réglementation; képi SD bleu-gris d'un général FAA, avec cocarde nationale, attaches dorées et visière soutachée. Une barrette d'épaule indiquant le rang est fixée à l'avant de la poche gauche; écusson de qualification de pilote de grade supérieur au-dessus de la poche gauche; ceinturon et baudrier avec étui de pistolet sans rabat. G2 combinaison de camouflage d'une pièce; LBE en nylon Tempex avec poches de nylon doubles pour mitraillette PA3; bottes de cuir noir FAA. G3 Veste doublée de molleton et pantalons réglementaires; doublure en nylon matelassée et épais pullover réglementaire. Lunettes attachées au képi à fourrure; bottes thermiques à lourdes semelles. G4 Veste de vol M1A1 avec insigne de bataillon sur la partie supérieure de la manche droite. Combinaison de vol US CWU-27 et casque US SPH-4C.

H1 Ecusson de manche de Groupe de Commando Amphibie. H2 Emblème de reconnaissance. H3 Ecusson de manche, 2nd Bataillon de l'Infanterie de Marine, 25e Régiment d'Infanterie. H5 Ecusson de manche, 25e Régiment d'Infanterie. H6 Insigne de rang en vinyle rouge sur fond vert olive. H7 Ecusson de béret de Commando de l'Armée. H8 Chevron de rang pour autres grades FAA. H9 Ecusson de béret de la Marine. H10 Ecusson de manche, 1ère Batterie AA de la Marine. H11 Ecusson de béret GOE. H12 Ecusson de béret ECCO. H13 Ailes de parachutiste d'OR de couleur sobre.

FAL SLR argentinischer Bauart. US M1-Helm mit Helmschutz nach argentinischer Art. A4 Olivgrüne Winterversion der Marineinfanterie/Marineuniform. Siehe Kruzifix am Stahlhelm und Rotkreuz-Abzeichen am linken Ärmel.

B1 US M1-Stahlhelm mit olivgrünem Helmschutz, angefertigt aus Feldjacken-Kapuze, und Schutzbrillen. Winter-Pelzhaube unter dem Helm. Wattierte Dubon-Parka, hergestellt in Israel. Grüne Standard-Armeeuniform, hohe schwarze Lederstiefel, faltbares Gewehr FN 50.61. Argentinische Tempex-Koppel und Munitionstaschen, spanische M5-Handgranate, grüner Nylonranzen, eingerollte Schlafmatratze. B2 Schwarze Kappe mit Esc Exp CBL 181-Abzeichen. Rangabzeichen auf Blusentasche aufgeknöpft. Tempex-Gürtel mit schwarzem US-Pistolenhalfter. B3 Tarnuniform, Feldweste mit Patronentaschen oben an der Brust, zwei M67-Granaten in kleinen Taschen. Grüne Wollkappe des Armeekommandos mit Emailabzeichen. Tempex-Koppel mit 9mm Browning in HalfterRollkragenpullover und Marineinfanterie-Stiefel. Bewaffnet mit faltbarem Gewehr FAL 50.63.

C1 Marineinfanterie-Tarnuniform mit aufsteckbaren Rangabzeichen in Rot und Blau auf den Schulterspangen. Olivgrüne Pelz-Wintermütze, Browning–Pistole, Gewehr FAL 50.63, Marineinfanterie-Stiefel. C2 Deser MAG-Schütze trägt grüne Standarduniform, gestrickte Wollkappe und Tempex-Koppel. Zwei spanische M5-Granaten und US-Kompaßtasche. 7,62mm Patronengurte und Browning in Halfter. C3 Sanitäterabzeichen auf Helmschutz, einfaches Rotkreuzabzeichen oben am linken Ärmel. Sanitärranzen ist ein Marineinfanterie–Rucksack mit aufgemaltem Roten Kreuz. Wundverbände in blauem Plastikbehälter, Winter-Feldjacke.

D1 Ungewöhnliche Feldweste mit großen Vordertaschen, Verbandstasche vorn links, integrierter Pistolenhalfter. Siehe unten links Pistoleinmunitionstaschen. Zwei M67-Granaten an einer Schnur um die Hüften, einteiliger Marineinfanterie-Overall mit Rangabzeichen an jeder Kragenseite. Schutzbrillen nach US-Art, amerikanischer M1-Helm mit argentinischem Helmschutz mit Tarnlaub-Einsteckband aus Gummirohr. Siehe Tarnhalstuch im amerikanischen "Duckhunter"-Stil. D2 Olivgrüne Standard-Armeefelduniform mit goldenen Rangabzeichen eines Offiziers im Generalsrang an den Kragenspitzen. Darüber trägt er eine wattierte Jacke bester Qualität, wollgefütterte Baumwollhandschuhe und ein Generalsbaton mit Silberpitz. D3 Israelische Parka, olivgrüne Felduniform, altaussehende Kartentasche und Feldstecher. Rang durch Brustabzeichen angezeigt; zwei M67-Granaten, ein argentinisches Funksprechgerät. Grüne Samtkappe mit gekreuzten Gewehren auf dem Abzeichen und der Nummer 25 in Goldfaden. D4 Olivgrüne Felduniform, PM-Armband am linken Ärmel, weißer Helmstreifen mit schwarzer Aufschrift.

E1 Grünes Lederriemenzeug: Koppel, Taschen, Bajonett FAL A mit Leder-Bajonettschlaufe, alte Aluminiumfeldflasche mit Segeltuchhülle, Joch- und Armzubehör. E2 Spaten nach deutscher Art mit Hülle. E3 Faltschaufel und Hülle nach US-Art. E5 Zusammengerollter Poncho und Zeltteil in Ledertragriemen. E6 Pistole Modell 1909 in Lederschlaufe. E7 .45 Pistole. E8 Doppeltasche für Pistolenmagazine. E9 Doppeltasche für MG-Magazine. E11 Behälter f. Gewehrgranaten-Zielgerät. E12 Wundverband in Plastikbehälter. E13 Braune Leder-Kartenmappe. E15 Säbelgurt f. Offizier. E16 Grüne Leder-Gewehrschlinge.

F1 Nylon-Riemenzeug mit FAL-Taschen, ein FAL-Bajonett Typ C, Tempex-Version eines US-Faltwerkzeugs. F2 Nylon-Munitionstasche f. Maschinenpistole. F3 Plastik-Feldflasche m. wattierter Nylonhülle. F4 Gasmaske und Behälter. F5 Amerikanische M17-Gasmaske. F6 Nylon-Rucksack. F7 Nylontasche f. Kompaß u. Pistolenmagazin. F9 Gewehrreinigungsmaterial. F10 Nylon-Tragreimen; US-Tarnzeltteil. F11 Nylon-Kompaßtasche. F12 Altmodische Marineinfanterie-Gurten und Koppel. 13 Rucksack. F14 Nylon-Gewehrschlaufe. F15 Erster Wundverband.

G1 Späte olivgrüne Felduniform; Blaugraue SD-Kappe eines FAA-Generals, mit argentinischer Kokarde, Goldbesatz und Bortenschirm. Rangabzeichen auf linker Tasche; Sam Brown-Gürtel m. offenem Pistolenhalfter, Pilotenabzeichen über linker Tasche. G2 Einteiliger Tarn-Overall; Nylon-Tempex LBE mit zwei Nylontaschen f. PA3-Maschinenpistolenmagazine; schwarze FAA-Lederstiefel. G3 FAA-Jacke, pelzgefüttert, und Hose; wattierte Nylonjacke und dicker Pullover. Schutzbrillen auf pelzgefütterter Kappe; warme Stiefel mit dicken Sohlen. G4 M1A1-Fliegerjacke mit Bataillonsabzeichen oben am rechten Ärmel. US-Fliegeranzug CWU-27 und US-Helm SPH-4C.

H1 Ärmelabzeichen, Amphibische Kommandogruppe. H2 Erkennungszeichen. H3 Ärmelabzeichen, 2. Marineinfanterie-Bataillon. H4 Kappenabzeichen, 25. Infanterieregiment. H5 Ärmelabzeichen, 25. Infanterieregiment. H6 Rangabzeichen, rote Vinyl auf olivgrünem Stoff. H7 Armee-Kommandokappen-Abzeichen. H8 FAA-Rangabzeichen-Winkel f. andere Ränge. H9 Marineinfanterie-Kappenabzeichen. 10 Ärmelabzeichen, 1. Marineinfanterie-AA-Batterie. H11 GOE-Kappenabzeichen. H12 ECCO-Kappenabzeichen. H13 Gedämpfte OR-Fallschirmjägerschwinge.